Liz

LARISSA BRANIN

COURAGE
BOOKS

PAGE 2 *The Burtons (pictured here with Michael Wilding, Jr., Maria Burton, Liza Todd, and a bodyguard) were not your everyday family, but the couple managed to devote as much time as possible to the children.*

PAGE 3 *It's hard to believe Elizabeth ever had any doubt about her looks. Yet early in her career, she considered Ava Gardner and Vivien Leigh to be actresses of true beauty. Indeed they were, but it is Taylor's face that has most often been heralded as the embodiment of beauty.*

OPPOSITE *Elizabeth as high-class prostitute Gloria Wandrous in Butterfield 8 (1960).*

PAGE 6 *Although Elizabeth's early studio image was that of the consummate glamor queen, the free-spirited mood of the early 1970s allowed Taylor to display the earthy quality only friends and family knew she had.*

©2000 by Michael Friedman Publishing Group, Inc.
First Published in the United States in 2000 by Courage Books
All rights reserved under the Pan-American and International Copyright Conventions

Printed by Hong Kong by Sing Cheong Printing Company Ltd.

10 9 8 7 6 5 4 3 2 1

Digit on the right indicates the number of this printing

Library of Congress Cataloging-in-Publication Data available upon request

ISBN 0-7624-0774-3

Liz
was prepared and produced by
Michael Friedman Publishing Group, Inc.
15 West 26th Street
New York, New York 10010

Editor: Ann Kirby
Art Director: Jeff Batzli
Design: Lindgren/Fuller Design
Photography Editor: Erin Feller
Production Manager: Camille Lee

This book may be ordered by mail from the publisher. *But try your bookstore first!*

Published by Courage Books, an imprint of
Running Press Book Publishers
125 South Twenty-second Street
Philadelphia, Pennsylvania 19103-4399

Visit us on the web!
www.runningpress.com

CONTENTS

INTRODUCTION

"I've been through it all baby, I'm Mother Courage."

—Elizabeth Taylor

Elizabeth Taylor's life story is undeniably compelling. Both tragedy and triumph have visited frequently. She was a precocious, pampered child star at the tender age of twelve. By the time she was twenty-six she had been married three times, was a widowed mother of three, and was about to become a notorious home wrecker. Her thirties were marked by a scandalous love triangle, two more marriages, two Academy Awards, various life-threatening illnesses, and fabulous wealth. Her later years were marred by drug and alcohol addiction, failed marriages, and more serious illnesses. But just when it looked as if it was all over, Elizabeth made a stunning comeback on Broadway, sobered up, and became a lucrative entrepreneur, finally garnering international acclaim not only as the grande dame of American cinema, but as one of the foremost crusaders against the AIDS epidemic. Throughout all this her striking beauty, famous flashing violet eyes, and penchant for jewels never flagged. It is this glamorous allure coupled with her genuine "passion for life" and seemingly indestructible nature that makes her story so fascinating.

OPPOSITE *Taylor, circa 1987.*

CHAPTER ONE

A Star in the Making

Francis and Sara Taylor welcomed a second child, Elizabeth Rosemond Taylor, into their fashionable world on February 27, 1932. The couple, expatriate Americans from the Midwest, had moved to London in 1927 when Francis accepted a management post at his wealthy uncle's art gallery. Sara and Francis had known each other as children in Kansas but it wasn't until meeting again in New York, where the former Sara Sothern was enjoying some acclaim as a Broadway actress, that the two became romantically involved. After they married in 1926, Sara fulfilled a commitment to act in one more play and then gave up the stage forever. Shortly afterward, the newlyweds headed across the Atlantic for London, where they lived quite stylishly, thanks to Francis's uncle Howard Young, who remained at his art gallery in New York.

PAGE 10 *One of the publicity photos promoting Elizabeth's 1944 book,* Nibbles and Me, *which was devoted to the antics of her beloved chipmunk, Nibbles (pictured).*

PAGE 11 *A still from Elizabeth's first film,* There's One Born Every Minute *(1943) with Carl Switzer, who was immortalized as Alfalfa in the* Our Gang *series. Elizabeth later summed up her character as "a beastly child who runs around slinging rubber bands at fat ladies' bottoms."*

Elizabeth and her older brother Howard were both beautiful children, but it was Elizabeth who startled people most with her delicate, dark looks.

In 1929 the Taylors' first child was born. Howard was a beautiful golden-haired baby. Indeed, his stunning looks prompted his giddy mother to remark that he looked "just like a Botticelli angel." During her next pregnancy two years later, Sara desperately hoped for a girl of equal beauty. While her wish to have a girl was granted, the infant's looks at birth caused immediate anxiety. Elizabeth had been born covered with thick, black hair—the result of a glandular condition known as hypertrichosis. Much to her family's relief, however, the unsightly condition disappeared within weeks after her birth. All that remained of her former pelt was the jet-black hair framing a creamy complexion and the dark eyebrows and thick lashes surrounding large, sparkling eyes.

Elizabeth's early years in England were indeed an idyllic time. The Taylors were befriended by Victor Cazalet, a dashing member of Parliament and a major

Howard, Sara, and Elizabeth in 1937. As a young girl, Elizabeth's cool composure and mature, steady gaze unnerved many, but Howard kept his little sister in place by calling her "Lizzie the Lizard." To this day, she has an aversion to the oft-used nickname, "Liz."

figure in London society. Cazalet even offered the Taylors a weekend manor house on his estate in the English countryside, which they frequented. Elizabeth and her brother, Howard, were surrounded by affluence. They spent many days at the sea on holiday with their mother and were catered to and coddled by servants. Elizabeth's first two Christmases and birthdays were spent in America, where the Taylors visited with family in Kansas and California before heading to Florida to luxuriate at Uncle Howard's sunny retreat. Everywhere the children went, they were fussed over for their beautiful appearance. Elizabeth was a particular favorite of Victor Cazalet. When she was four he gave her a mare named Betty, which she rode bareback at their weekend retreat. It was during this period that her famous rapport with animals became most apparent; she was the only rider Betty would tolerate without a struggle.

By early 1939 the crushing threat of war in Europe sent the Taylors back to America. Their destination was Pasadena, California, where Sara's father now owned a chicken ranch. It seemed natural that Sara wanted to be with her family in California, but it is often assumed that the former actress already had Hollywood ambitions for her children. After a brief stay in Pasadena, Francis Taylor moved the family to the tony Pacific Palisades and later to Beverly Hills, where the art gallery had been relocated. It wasn't long before the gallery was attracting a celebrated clientele, including one of Hollywood's premier gossip columnists, Hedda Hopper.

An acquaintance of Victor Cazalet, Hopper helped spread the word about the fine pieces to be found in Francis's gallery. Not one to miss such an opportunity, Sara quickly introduced Hopper to Elizabeth with the hope that the influential columnist, a former actress herself, could help get her daughter into pictures. Hopper was indeed struck by Taylor's breathtaking beauty, but later wrote that she had to endure a rather uncomfortable moment listening to a reluctant Elizabeth sing on her mother's command.

During her first few years in California, Elizabeth had a brief encounter with a normal childhood. She attended school, was teased about her British accent, and played outside with friends, many of whom were the

Producers weren't quite sure what to do with Elizabeth—her beautiful looks and seeming aloofness, which was actually acute shyness, made it hard to cast her in typical little girl roles.

Elizabeth tries her best to strike a genuine child star pose, but her ethereal features made her difficult to cast.

A Star Among Child Stars

In the early to mid-1930s, Shirley Temple epitomized the ultimate child star. Her beribboned golden curls, dimpled cheeks, and effervescent song-and-dance routines dazzled and cheered moviegoers during the Great Depression. Although Temple was the crown jewel of Paramount Studios, MGM had the lion's share of child stars. Among its impressive roster the studio boasted Jackie Coogan, Freddie Bartholomew, Mickey Rooney, and Judy Garland. For a brief time MGM even had the young soprano sensation Deanna Durbin.

Deanna Durbin (left), as she appeared in Universal's Three Smart Girls, *a blockbuster that brought the financially strapped studio out of the red and kick-started Durbin's dizzying rise to fame.*

Durbin was featured in a 1936 MGM short with Garland to showcase their musical talents. Legend has it that MGM studio head Louis B. Mayer wanted to "drop the fat one" (Garland) but due to a studio mixup, it was Durbin who ended up without a contract. While Garland began her steady rise to phenomenal fame at MGM, Durbin was signed on by the financially strapped Universal Studios, which quickly placed her in a starring role in *Three Smart Girls* (1936). The musical was a box-office smash and was the first of a series of similar Universal vehicles highlighting Durbin's amazing operatic voice and celluloid charm.

Hollywood gossip columnist Hedda Hopper visiting Elizabeth on the set of Giant. *The two shared a warm friendship until Elizabeth's love life took a scandalous turn.*

Durbin's popularity at the box office saved Universal Studios from bankruptcy and she was soon given the studio sobriquet "the mortgage lifter." By the age of fourteen she was the highest paid woman in the world, earning upwards of $400,000 per film. Like Shirley Temple, however, Durbin's popularity began to wane as she matured. By the time the nine-year-old Elizabeth Taylor had signed on with Universal Studios in 1942, ticket sales for Durbin were faltering and she was placed in dramas.

Sara Taylor envisioned Elizabeth as the next Deanna Durbin and even prompted her nervous child to sing a rather warbled tune for the influential gossip columnist Hedda Hopper. It was Elizabeth's stunning looks, however, that got both Hopper's and Universal's attention. After one forgettable film, Universal dropped Taylor when a studio executive barked that she couldn't act or sing and called her mother "unbearable." MGM, meanwhile, was unwittingly poised to make up for its earlier loss of Durbin to Universal by taking a chance on the discarded "no talent" Taylor.

Elizabeth signing her MGM contract for her breakthrough role as Priscilla, the daughter of a British aristocrat in Lassie Come Home *in 1943. At the time, Lassie earned more per week than Elizabeth—but that would soon change!*

children of Hollywood stars. In 1941, however, nine-year-old Elizabeth's life began to move along a different path. She had landed a six-month studio contract with Universal, thanks to Sara's blossoming friendship with the wife of the studio chairman. While Sara was overjoyed about the contract, Elizabeth was disappointed. She wanted to work for MGM.

At the time, Universal Studios' major star, Deanna Durbin, was no longer the box-office smash she had once been. A child star with amazing operatic talents, Durbin had single-handedly brought the studio out of the red with her first film, *Three Smart Girls* (1936), and continued to reign as studio queen in block-

In this 1946 Courage of Lassie *still Elizabeth, pictured with Frank Morgan, displays the genuine nurturing skills that were among her defining qualities. Behind the scenes, however, tensions were rising at home over Elizabeth's lack of a normal childhood and her role as the family's major breadwinner.*

buster after blockbuster. Perhaps styles had changed in wartime America, but it's more likely that Durbin's maturity and marriage in 1941 were major factors in her declining appeal. As Shirley Temple and countless other child stars discovered, growing up was something that their audience—and studios—could not tolerate. Durbin was relegated to dramatic roles and, though still a marvelous singing talent, never regained her former popularity. Universal was looking for a new star.

OPPOSITE *A seventeen-year-old Elizabeth tends to the weekly chore of bathing her cocker spaniel, Amy (named after Taylor's character in* Little Women) *in an MGM publicity shot. Although the studios were known to embellish their stars' lives for the sake of good press, Elizabeth's affinity for animals was genuine.*

While the studio no doubt had high hopes for Elizabeth, these were quickly dashed. Not sure what to do with the young actress, the studio promptly placed her in a ridiculous farce, *There's One Born Every Minute* (1942). The vehicle was intended to resuscitate the flagging career of yet another maturing child star, Carl Switzer, who was immortalized (and forever typecast) as Alfalfa in the famous *Our Gang* series. The picture bombed and Taylor—who couldn't sing or dance to the studio's satisfaction—was swiftly dropped from her contract after a studio executive dismissed her as talentless and further complained that she did not have the face of a child because her eyes were "too old." Elizabeth and her mother were crushed.

After her good showing as Priscilla in Lassie Come Home, *Elizabeth was again featured with Roddy McDowall in* The White Cliffs of Dover. *The studio, however, did not go out on a limb to display Taylor's talents in this film, since her screen time was even shorter than it was in* Lassie.

Back to a more normal childhood routine, the resilient Elizabeth resumed her earlier friendships, while Sara continued plotting to get her daughter another chance. But it was Francis Taylor who secured his daughter's big break. During the war, Francis had gone on night patrol with another member of his civilian unit, MGM producer Samuel Marx. "Elizabethan" lore has it that Francis casually brought up his daughter's name when Marx mentioned his trouble finding a child with a British accent for a role in the upcoming movie *Lassie Come Home* (1943). A television interview with Marx in later years, however, painted a slightly different picture. He laughingly recalled that, as with most Hollywood parents, Frances constantly badgered him about his beautiful daughter until finally Marx agreed to see her.

Marx claimed to have almost passed out upon first encountering the dazzling young Elizabeth. He recalled that she arrived hand in hand with her mother, wearing a purple velvet dress with matching cap; he described her as having "purple eyes." At this age, Elizabeth resembled an exquisite doll and exuded a quiet dignity well beyond her years. Aside from her looks, Marx was also pleased with her British accent and the fact that she was shorter than Roddy McDowall, the star of *Lassie Come Home*. MGM signed her up in 1943 with a guarantee of one hundred dollars a week per year, 10 percent of which went to her mother as chaperone. Elizabeth Taylor was on her way to forging a career with the most prestigious movie studio in the world.

OPPOSITE *Elizabeth playfully chases former co-star Roddy McDowall on Malibu Beach. Theirs was no studio-fabricated friendship: throughout all the marriages, divorces, scandals, and tragedies to come, Elizabeth could always rely on her childhood friend.*

CHAPTER TWO

The MGM Years

When Elizabeth first walked onto the set of her first MGM movie, *Lassie Come Home* (1943), the film's equally young star, Roddy McDowall—who was to become Elizabeth's close, lifelong friend—claimed to have laughed in disbelief upon seeing her:

> *It was like seeing a tiny adult walking up with this exquisite face. She was the most beautiful child I ever saw. Her coloring was amazing. Her eyes were so astounding that the cameraman asked if her mother would have the mascara removed. Elizabeth said "I'm not wearing any."*

Indeed, Taylor was well suited for her small role in *Lassie Come Home* as Priscilla, the beautiful daughter of a wealthy English duke. And her screen presence was not lost on MGM executives. Not only did the movie became a box-office

A typical MGM-generated "candid" photo of the stars at play. Here, Jane Powell (left) poses as the host of an outdoor barbecue for her pals, including Roddy McDowall and Elizabeth. Elizabeth's bathing suit somewhat contradicts the studio's effort to portray their young stars as all-American, wholesome teens.

PAGE 22 Elizabeth's role in National Velvet as the determined English schoolgirl who wins a racehorse and gets a former jockey (Mickey Rooney) to help her enter and win the Grand National, is still hailed as one of her best performances.

PAGE 23 Taylor as she appeared in Suddenly, Last Summer, the film version of Tennessee Williams' disturbing play. Although she turned in one of her best performances, in her private life, Elizabeth was still reeling from the bad press over her adulterous affair with Eddie Fisher, whom she had recently wed.

smash, but it prompted studio head Louis B. Mayer (a sentimentalist who reportedly had tears streaming down his face after a *Lassie* screening) to make more "family fare" films with animal themes.

In the meantime, the studio's next move was to loan out Taylor to Twentieth Century-Fox to play a small yet significant role as an ethereal schoolgirl named Helen Burns in the moody *Jane Eyre* (1944). Taylor displayed an eerie maturity in the film. Her character endured having her hair (a wig) chopped off, marching around stoically in a chilly downpour, and acting out a death scene. It was quite an impressive performance for an eleven-year-old. Taylor was next cast in a tiny part in the elaborate MGM–Irene Dunne production *The White Cliffs of Dover* (1944), which also featured Roddy McDowall.

That same year, MGM bought the rights for the best-selling book *National Velvet* and began casting for the film. The story revolved around a girl

named Velvet Brown, the daughter of a Sussex butcher, who wins a racehorse named Pi in a raffle. The young girl then teams up with a former jockey in the area (Mickey Rooney) and, disguised as a male jockey, enters and wins England's prestigious Grand National. Elizabeth, with the full support of her mother, was determined to land the plum role of Velvet, but there was one problem: Velvet Brown was supposed to be on the brink of puberty and Elizabeth was a petite twelve-year-old. She was considered too young, too short, and (ironically, given her later development) not physically well endowed.

Legend has it that Elizabeth strode into the casting director's office and confidently announced, "I am going to play Velvet." She set out like an Olympian in training—eating huge meals, getting plenty of sleep, and maintaining a rigorous exercise regimen, which included chest-developing exercises and even the use of "fast-grow" creams. Ninety days later a triumphant Elizabeth showed up at *National Velvet* producer Pandro S. Berman's office. She was a few inches taller and was wearing a tight red sweater, clearly revealing the bit of maturity needed for the part. Elizabeth was now Velvet Brown and her subsequent passionate performance made her an overnight sensation. Louis B. Mayer was ecstatic. In fact, he was so gratified by her performance in this wildly successful "family fare" film, that he agreed to give Elizabeth the racehorse Pi (a.k.a. King Charles) after filming. In addition, Elizabeth was awarded a bonus of $7,500 and a new seven-year contract was drawn up, with a starting salary of $300 a week.

Meanwhile, Sara Taylor was garnering a reputation as a nuisance on the set. She made a habit of sitting right behind the camera, giving Elizabeth pointers as she acted. Sara developed an intricate system of hand signals to communicate

to Elizabeth how to improve her performance. When Elizabeth wasn't being coached on the set, she was being schooled between fittings and shoots at MGM's famous Little Red Schoolhouse with other child stars, or posing for the publicity stills now in high demand. Girls everywhere began tacking up photos in their bedrooms of Elizabeth astride a horse or posing with one of her many pets.

In 1946 Elizabeth starred in *The Courage of Lassie*, a rather tepid film considering her recent success. Off the set, tensions were rising at home between Francis and Sara. Francis disapproved of Elizabeth's lack of a normal childhood and was uncomfortable with her role as the family's major breadwinner. In later years, Elizabeth matter-of-factly told an interviewer that her father drank too much and sometimes "batted her around." Although Francis complained, Sara was completely absorbed with moviedom and, since she was on the MGM payroll too, she would never consider giving it all up. Soon Francis

Although Elizabeth's fame and fortune initially caused a lot of strain on Francis and Sara's marriage, they were equally devoted to their daughter.

and son Howard began spending more time away, sometimes residing at the Beverly Hills Hotel or fishing in the country. By all accounts, Howard was a down-to-earth teen who rejected any notion of getting into pictures himself, even though he surely had the looks and the connections to do so. His disinterest was so genuine that when a screen test was set up against his will, he showed up with a shaved head.

Elizabeth was surprisingly inactive from the spring of 1945 through the summer of 1946 because the studio could not find a suitable script for its newest

Elizabeth in Life with Father, *which starred the dapper William Powell (left). Her role called for her to be little more than a charming, lovestruck adolescent, which she pulled off quite well considering that her parents separated during filming.*

star. Instead, the studio's publicity department kept Elizabeth in the news with photo layouts and interviews, including a *Life* magazine headline story just before her thirteenth birthday proclaiming, "Elizabeth Taylor Loves Animals and Out-of-doors." During this media blitz the oft-quoted myth was created about her "British-born father" rescuing her from a bombed-out England, where in earlier years she had danced in a command performance for the king and queen.

This idle period ended when she was loaned to Warner Bros. to play the daughter of William Powell and Irene Dunne in a screen adaptation of the Broadway hit *Life with Father* (1947). Her role was small and, for the most part, critics only noticed her beautiful face and her charm. What is significant about this film is what took place off camera. Sara was becoming increasingly obnoxious in her overcoddling of Elizabeth on the set. Fearful of drafts and concerned about overwork, Sara also began pulling Elizabeth off the set because of illnesses like sinus infections or sore throats, which no one—including Elizabeth—believed she suffered from. A studio executive later complained in a memo during filming that Elizabeth was a nervous, high-strung child and her condition caused many costly absences. Perhaps there was some truth to that, considering that her parents separated during filming. But it has been alleged in other biographies that it was because her mother was having an affair with the movie's director.

Seemingly overnight, Elizabeth made the transition from child star to screen siren without experiencing the usual awkward teenage years that had felled many before her. At fifteen Elizabeth had the body of a grown woman—a phenomenon not lost on many men around her, who stared at her in lusty disbelief. Louis B. Mayer, of course, did not approve of Elizabeth's use of makeup, gold hoop earrings, and revealing, Jennifer Jones–inspired peasant dresses. To accommodate her budding looks in a more wholesome way, Elizabeth was next cast in *Cynthia* (1947), a sweet film that included her first screen kiss and marked her move into mature roles.

The plot of *Cynthia* was similar to Taylor's own sequestered life at the time. The story concerns a frail young girl who breaks away from her overbearing, overprotective parents to attend a high school prom. Elizabeth turned in a very moving performance and the film was a great success. In real life, it wasn't just her parents who were overprotective of her—it was the studio as well. Elizabeth was like a beautiful princess kept behind protected walls. Her only contacts with the real world were essentially staged events for the benefit of publicity. In reality she spent about four hours working on the set, three hours

in the Little Red Schoolhouse, a few more hours back at work, and then went home, where Sara kept a vigilant eye on her.

Both of her parents were reportedly involved in extramarital affairs that were common knowledge among Hollywood insiders, which must have added to Elizabeth's own teenage angst. During this tumultuous time, Elizabeth was having romantic troubles of her own: she was suffering from a bout of unrequited love. The object of her affection was British newcomer Peter Lawford. Although the two were friendly and sometimes went out together, Lawford preferred lissome blond starlets over Elizabeth. He later conceded that Elizabeth had a beautiful face, but caustically likened her legs to "pods." She soon began to swim more and became more selective about what she ate—especially forgoing her favorite mint milkshakes.

At fifteen, Elizabeth settled into a string of fairly fluffy roles portraying beautiful young women, often daughters: *A Date With Judy* (1948), *Julia Misbehaves* (1948), and *Little Women* (1949). Her semicomedic performance in the latter as Amy, the beautiful and spoiled sister, stood out—not only because of her breathtaking, Technicolor beauty, but because the raven-haired star wore a long strawberry-blond wig. By 1950 Elizabeth's own youthful long dark locks were shorn into a very chic style that only enhanced her already mature appearance. This new look expedited her debut in *Conspirator* (1949) not just as an adult, but as the sexy British wife of thirty-eight-year-old matinee idol Robert Taylor. And just in case the audience didn't quite catch that little Velvet Brown was now a woman, she was filmed wearing a clingy black negligé, while embracing Robert Taylor during a bedroom scene. She was barely eighteen.

Little Women is a perfect example of MGM's lush family movies at their sentimental best. Elizabeth portrayed the self-obsessed sister Amy, managing to round out the harsh character with touches of warmth and humor.

OPPOSITE *Just a year after* Little Women, *Elizabeth's mature looks and figure brought her more adult roles. After playing a sexy wife in* Conspirator, *Elizabeth bragged (perhaps prematurely) that being kissed by Robert Taylor (left) would ensure she'd never be regarded as a teenybopper again.*

A Lifelong Love

Taylor's passionate portrayal of a girl devoted to her racehorse in *National Velvet* (1944) made her a superstar at the age of twelve. Immediately, the MGM publicity department began churning out stories offering fans everything they might ever want to know about Elizabeth Taylor. As often happened in those days, facts were interwoven with fiction to the star's advantage. Although Taylor was indeed born in England and had traces of a British accent in her early years, press releases focused on her connections to British gentry rather than her parents' origins in unglamorous Kansas. One thing MGM never had to fabricate, however, was Elizabeth's deep love of animals.

Fan magazines focused on this gentle aspect of Elizabeth's personality and her growing menagerie was often featured in stories. In 1944, with the studio's help, a book devoted to Elizabeth's relationship with her famous pet chipmunk, Nibbles, was published. Elizabeth purportedly took her role as the authoress of *Nibbles and Me* quite seriously. The result was a fluffy chronicle of her adventures with Nibbles the chipmunk. Of course, the studio used the book as free publicity for her upcoming role in *The Courage of Lassie*. Inside, readers were treated to various photographs of the movie (which was originally titled *Blue Sierra*) in production.

To this day, Elizabeth is often pictured with a dog on her arm or in her lap. In the fifties, she seemed to prefer French poodles. Today, her constant canine companion is a white Maltese named Sugar.

Elizabeth was never without a furry companion of some sort. When she bought her first "Hollywood-style" home with second husband Michael Wilding, some people (including Wilding) were shocked to discover Elizabeth's penchant for letting her sometimes destructive animals have the run of the house.

After *The Big Hangover* (1950), a stale comedy with Van Johnson, Elizabeth was back on familiar ground playing the beautiful daughter of Spencer Tracy and Joan Bennett in *Father of the Bride* (1950). As Kay, Taylor effectively turns the lives of her "Moms" and "Pops" upside down with the sudden announcement of her engagement. The fact that Elizabeth herself was to marry hotel heir Conrad "Nicky" Hilton just weeks after filming made the scenes in which her character struggles with conflicting emotions over entering marital bliss and remaining Daddy's little girl all the more poignant.

The movie was a box-office smash and the wedding day sequences showing off a radiant Taylor in a lacy bridal gown served as a teaser for her own pending nuptials. Perhaps hoping to dish up another teaser for real-life events, post-honeymoon Taylor was promptly placed in *Father of the Bride*'s fruitful sequel, *Father's Little Dividend* (1951). Her next film was *A Place in the Sun* (1951), a Paramount Studio remake of *An American Tragedy* (1931). The film was actually shot in 1949, but due to director George Stevens's meticulous editing process, it took well over a year for the film to be released. When it finally premiered, audiences and critics alike marveled at the sizzling cinematic chemistry between Taylor and the brilliant Actor's Studio–trained star, Montgomery Clift.

Elizabeth and Montgomery Clift made an impossibly beautiful pair in A Place in the Sun. *Taylor's performance, which benefited from Clift's subtle guidance, met with much critical acclaim.*

OPPOSITE *Elizabeth as the glowing bride, accompanied by Spencer Tracy, in 1950's* Father of the Bride. *MGM assigned its house designer to create Elizabeth's gown for the film, as well as the one she would wear in her real-life wedding soon after it was released. The two dresses were predictably similar.*

The two stars became fast friends while working on location at Lake Tahoe. Clift even began giving an eager Taylor some acting tips he had picked up from the Actor's Studio. The role of Angela Vickers could have very easily fallen into Taylor's heretofore stereotypical "beautiful rich girl" mold, but the combination of her affinity with Clift and the expert direction by Stevens prompted Elizabeth to turn in a dynamic performance. The smoldering love scenes were so realistic that rumors circulated in the gossip columns that the two were actually in love during filming. In Elizabeth's case, that may have been true. Clift, however, was homosexual, and if Taylor was unaware of this when she first met him, she soon found out. In any case, it was during the filming of *A Place in the Sun* that Taylor announced her engagement to Nicky Hilton.

All in a day's work! Elizabeth laughs at her appearance during a morning shampoo at the studio.

Despite her stunning performance, MGM again dropped the ball and resumed placing Taylor in lackluster roles that for the most part merely cashed in on her looks. She was placed in extravagant and lush features such as *Ivanhoe* (1952), *Beau Brummel* (1954), and *Elephant Walk* (1954), but it wasn't until another loan-out, this time for the Warner Bros. epic *Giant* (1956), that she scored a hit and reached another acting milestone.

Behind the radiant smile, Elizabeth was distraught after her divorce from Hilton. Living on her own for the first time, Elizabeth told a visiting Hedda Hopper that she was happy, "but not nineteen happy."

Taylor convincingly aged about thirty years as Leslie Benedict, the beautiful Virginian bride of Bick Benedict (Rock Hudson), the scion of a rich ranching family in Texas. Taken from the lush fields of Virginia to the vast, dusty Texas ranch run by her surly sister-in-law, Leslie struggles to come to terms with her new life and growing family. Taylor displayed a convincing range of emotions: tenderness and steeliness; intelligence and stubbornness; childishness and maturity.

The film also starred the mercurial James Dean, who at twenty-four was already an acting legend after making only two films. As the awkward ranch hand in love with Leslie,

A still promoting the cinematic slap Elizabeth receives in Elephant Walk. Taylor replaced Vivien Leigh, who fell ill at the beginning of production. Elizabeth was chosen because she had the same coloring as Leigh, of whom some long shots remained in the film.

Dean shared a number of scenes with Taylor. As with Montgomery Clift, Taylor developed an intense relationship with Dean off the set. Most of the cast were still working on the picture when news came in late September that Dean, who had completed all his scenes a few days earlier, had been killed instantly in a car collision on the way to a racing competition. Elizabeth was devastated and could not work for days. When she did return to the set, she was still teary and resented George Stevens for making her work under such conditions.

OPPOSITE *During the filming of Giant, Elizabeth developed a deep friendship with James Dean. Always sensitive to others' pain, Elizabeth reached out to the troubled Dean, and the two formed a close bond. When Dean was killed in a car crash shortly after finishing his scenes, she was inconsolable.*

Giant co-star Rock Hudson helps Elizabeth plant her handprints in front of Grauman's Chinese Theatre in Hollywood. The two shared a life-long friendship, which she said began after they invented a chocolate martini one late night off the set of Giant.

A revealing shot of Elizabeth from Raintree County. Elizabeth had to lose weight for the film, as she had begun to turn to food to console her in times of personal crisis.

After the success of *Giant*, which was enhanced by Dean's brilliant performance, Taylor was cast in *Raintree County* (1957) with Montgomery Clift. This saga about a beautiful southern belle who loses her mind was beautifully filmed and costumed but was rather dark and overwrought. Yet Taylor shined throughout with her sensitive portrayal of the doomed Susanna Drake and garnered her first Academy Award nomination. The film also marked Taylor's first time feigning a very authentic-sounding Southern accent, which she would use to great effect in later films.

Sadly, *Raintree County* proved less fortuitous for Montgomery Clift. On the first day of shooting, after leaving a party at Elizabeth's home, Clift got into a near-fatal car accident not far down the road. Elizabeth rushed outside and held her unconscious friend's head in her lap until medical help arrived. It took nine weeks for Clift to heal from a badly broken jaw and nose. When filming resumed, not only were his previously chiseled features marred, but the inner fire he once displayed seemed to be flickering out. There was something missing both on- and offscreen. The sad vacancy was painful to witness, especially for Elizabeth. Clift had been struggling with drugs before the accident, but now his addiction grew worse. He became dependent on the drugs—first to ease his physical pain and later his mental anguish. Taylor not only saved his life that fateful night by deftly pulling his bloody, broken teeth out of his throat, she remained supportive of him for the rest of his short life.

In 1958 Elizabeth reached another career milestone with her stunning performance as Maggie the Cat in *Cat on a Hot Tin Roof*, which earned her a second Oscar nomination for best actress. It was during the shooting of this sultry screen adaptation of the Tennessee Williams play that the biggest tragedy in Elizabeth's life occurred. Her third husband, Mike Todd, was killed in a plane crash (see Chapter Three). Todd had felt that the complicated Maggie the Cat was the best role that Elizabeth had ever been offered, so after a month of mourning, Taylor stoically resumed shooting "for Mike."

OPPOSITE Raintree County was a sweeping epic, an attempt by MGM to outdo Gone with the Wind. Clift's performance suffered from his personal troubles, but his and Elizabeth's friendship never faltered.

No doubt it was a cathartic experience, and she released a fiery energy never before exhibited. It was as if Taylor were letting all the inner rage and anguish she felt over her husband's death spill out onto the screen, leaving her raw and exposed. Movie audiences now proclaimed Elizabeth Taylor the biggest star in America. Then another event in her life helped alter her screen image from beautiful heroine to red-hot mama—her controversial affair with Todd's best friend, Eddie Fisher. Not only was Taylor still figuratively wearing her widow's weeds, but Fisher was married to MGM good girl Debbie Reynolds (see Chapter Three).

The ensuing public backlash and voyeuristic fascination over their illicit affair was intense. Rather than try to cover up or neutralize the scandal, MGM cashed in on Taylor's notoriety by promoting ultra-sexy trailers of Taylor as Maggie the Cat in virtual heat. There was even a line in the film in which she yells, "Skipper is dead and I am *alive!*"—which mirrored what she reportedly told Hedda Hopper at the height of her Fisher affair. In fact, Hopper later wrote that

Taylor really said, "What do you expect me to do—sleep alone?" Hopper felt this reply was unprintable so she instead had Taylor cry out, "Mike is dead and I'm alive"—a line the public no doubt later recognized in the movie. Hopper had always been a strong ally of Taylor's, but after the Taylor-Fisher-Reynolds triangle, she was indignant and wrote a scathing column condemning Elizabeth as a wanton home wrecker.

When things calmed down a bit, Taylor was featured in another Tennessee Williams vehicle, *Suddenly, Last Summer* (1959), in which she played opposite Montgomery Clift as yet another beautiful, albeit off-kilter woman. The film was noted for its excellent cinematography, disturbing theme, and superb ensemble cast, including Katharine Hepburn. But Taylor's complex portrayal of a tortured soul was what stood out most. At the end of the movie she delivers a wrenching, close-up monologue (which was twelve scripted pages long) that is cleverly intercut with scenes of the horrible memory she is recalling. After two days of shooting this monologue, Taylor collapsed on the set in

ABOVE *After spending a year at the center of the Eddie Fisher maelstrom, a seductively posed Elizabeth manages to look very well rested and undisturbed on the outdoor set of* Suddenly, Last Summer.

Regardless of Elizabeth's low opinion of Butterfield 8, *she beamed as she held her Oscar next to fellow winner Burt Lancaster, who won for his performance in* Elmer Gantry. *Elizabeth maintained that she had only won because she had almost died of pneumonia. Best actress nominee Shirley MacLaine agreed, exclaiming, "I lost to a tracheotomy!"*

tears and remained in bed for two days. This powerhouse performance earned her a third consecutive Academy Award nomination. Elizabeth has said *Suddenly, Last Summer* is her favorite film and "the greatest, the most emotionally draining, the most emotionally stimulating professional experience of my life."

Despite three back-to-back Oscar nominations, she did not receive the coveted statue until her final picture under contract with MGM, *Butterfield 8* (1960). Elizabeth personally hated the film, in which she portrayed a high-class prostitute, but was forced into doing it because she still owed MGM another picture. What made Taylor all the more eager to get out of this deal was the fact that she had just signed a landmark contract with Twentieth Century Fox to star in *Cleopatra* (1963). After completing the hated *Butterfield 8*, Elizabeth flew to a damp and chilly London to begin *Cleopatra*, but she soon contracted viral

A heated scene from Butterfield 8, which paled in comparison to Elizabeth's real-life outburst—she threw her shoes at the screen in disgust after viewing early rushes of the film.

Elizabeth looking literally like a million dollars as the Queen of the Nile. During early production of Cleopatra, *Elizabeth fell ill with respiratory ailments brought on by drafty conditions at the London studio. Her long recuperation necessitated the fateful move to Rome with new co-stars.*

Elizabeth is all smiles in 1959 as she shakes hands with Buddy Adler and Walter Wanger after signing an unprecedented contract to earn a guaranteed million dollars for her starring role in Cleopatra. *She also made the savvy decision to demand a right to film percentages, script changes, a European location, and luxurious accommodations.*

pneumonia and nearly died. An emergency tracheotomy was performed and all over the world, the public followed every temperature spike.

Once recovered from this near-death experience, she was forgiven all her previous sins and when the Oscars came around a month after her harrowing hospital stay, she won Best Actress for *Butterfield 8*. She approached the podium humbly, her fresh scar prominent, and thanked her peers in a childlike, shaky voice, but she still told anyone who listened that the film was garbage and maintained that she had only won because of the sympathy vote. But at that point Taylor didn't much care; she just wanted to get on with what was at the time the biggest deal ever made in movie history—a million-dollar contract to portray the Queen of the Nile.

CHAPTER THREE

Love and Marriages

Elizabeth approached the altar a total of eight times—twice with the same man—and each time, amid flashing bulbs and the whirl of movie cameras, she proclaimed her undying love and swore *this* was the one that would last. Several biographers and acquaintances have tried to explain away her marriage mania by claiming that Elizabeth "had to marry whomever she fell in love with." Elizabeth was indeed genuinely in love each and every time she said "I do," but a more plausible explanation for her multiple marriages may be the simple fact that her formative years on the studio lot were filled with make-believe and notions of idealized romance.

After all, the studio had paved the way for her in all aspects of life—including romance. It was the studio that promoted her first true romance, with All-American UCLA football star Glenn Davis. Elizabeth leapt into the

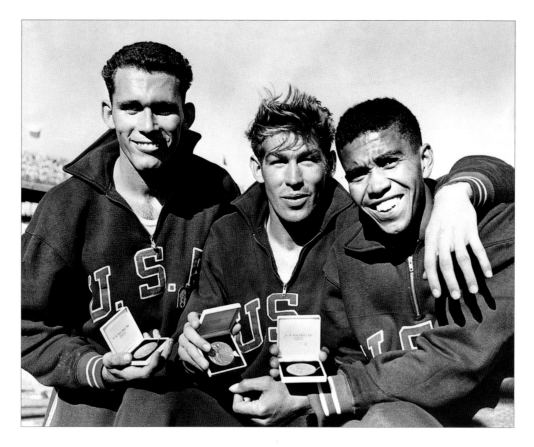

Elizabeth's made-for-Hollywood romance with UCLA football star Glenn Davis (center) was the stuff that movies were made of, but it didn't last long. Shortly after Davis returned from Korea, Elizabeth became engaged to William Pawley.

role wholeheartedly and had long been pining for a husband. For one thing, she saw marriage as a means of gaining her independence from her mother. Davis gave her the "going steady" tokens of that era—a football sweater and a school ring—which she wore with delight. When Davis was sent to Korea, Elizabeth melodramatically mourned his absence and spent her time faithfully writing him letters.

But it wasn't long until Elizabeth met someone else. After a shopping trip to Paris she spent her seventeenth birthday with her parents at Uncle Howard Young's Florida retreat. There Elizabeth met William Pawley, Jr., a handsome twenty-eight-year-old business executive and heir to a family fortune. When Davis returned from his military tour of Korea, he came to Florida to visit Elizabeth. Newspapers gushed that they were about to be engaged but Elizabeth later acknowledged it never went that far and that she was "never in love with Glenn." After a few chummy dates with Davis in Florida and later California, Elizabeth accepted a 3.5-carat diamond engagement ring from Pawley in the summer of 1949. Her family announced that the wedding would take place after her eighteenth birthday and that the happy couple planned to reside in Miami.

By summer's end, however, Elizabeth's excitement over being Mrs. Pawley of Miami began to wane and by mid-September the engagement was off. It has

PAGE 50 *Although the eighteen-year-old Elizabeth had Hollywood visions of the perfect marriage, one studio executive quipped wryly that Hilton "would make a nice first husband."*

PAGE 51 *Movie magazines relished stories about Elizabeth—especially when it came to her love life. In the more than forty years since this cover story was published, things have not changed!*

been hinted that Pawley was very conservative and did not want Elizabeth to act anymore or that his family disapproved of his marrying a movie star. But Elizabeth later summed it up breezily by stating, "We went well together under the palm trees; we looked nice on the dance floor; we loved to go boating; we had nothing in common."

During her subsequent filming of *A Place in the Sun* she met twenty-three-year-old Conrad Nicholas "Nicky" Hilton. He sought out an introduction to her and was soon ardently courting her and inviting the Taylors to stay at the family mansion in Bel-Air, their retreat at Lake Arrowhead, and the plush Hilton hotel at Arrowhead Springs. Dubbed America's most eligible bachelor, Nicky also had a reputation as a hard-drinking man-about-town. But he was able to keep this aspect of his personality in check during the courtship. Just before her eighteenth birthday, the Taylors announced that Elizabeth and Nicky were to be married on May 6 at the Church of the Good Shepherd in Los Angeles.

The wedding itself was an MGM production and everything from the bridesmaid dresses to the wedding cake were underwritten by L. B. Mayer, who presided over the affair as if he himself were the father of the bride. More than twenty-five hundred spectators jammed the streets to catch a glimpse of the newlyweds and their all-star guest list.

But the marriage was doomed from the start. Nicky reportedly spent his entire wedding night drinking and gambling, then left his new bride alone for much of their three-month European honeymoon. There were later insinuations that he even beat Taylor. Seven months after their extravagant nuptials, Elizabeth sued Nicky for divorce on the grounds of extreme mental cruelty. For months Elizabeth's silence over her domestic strife manifested itself in nervous tension and various illnesses—including a week-long hospital stay due to stomach pains. She later revealed, "I fell off my pink cloud with a thud."

The failure of the marriage left Elizabeth humiliated and disillusioned. For years the only thing she would say about the grim reality of their marriage was that she "didn't have one clue how to cope with it." Recently, however, Elizabeth spoke out for the first time about what caused her to seek a hasty divorce from Hilton. In an interview in *Talk* magazine, Taylor candidly told a reporter that a drunken Nicky kicked her in the stomach one night and caused her to lose a baby she had no idea she was carrying.

Immediately after the divorce, Elizabeth was starring in the ironically titled *Love Is Better Than Ever* (1952) and was soon indulging in an open affair with the film's director, twenty-six-year-old Stanley Donen. A former Broadway

After her tumultuous union with Hilton, Elizabeth welcomed settling down to a quieter life with the much-older and very worldly Michael Wilding.

dancer and choreographer, Donen was also married. Fearful of the public's wrath, MGM soon trundled Taylor off to England to star in *Ivanhoe* (1952).

The studio's move worked—to a certain degree. By the time filming ended, Taylor was madly in love again, this time with the popular British cinema star Michael Wilding, who was twenty years her senior and also married. After his divorce, he continued seeing Elizabeth in Hollywood. *She* finally proposed to *him*. (She affectionately dubbed him "Mr. Shilly-Shally.") Wilding initially thought they should wait until she was older, but Elizabeth persisted and he relented. Just a few days after her twentieth birthday, Taylor and Wilding were wed in a civil ceremony in London and were practically crushed by the frenzied mob outside. Eleven months later her first child, Michael Wilding, Jr., was born by emergency cesarean section. Although her recovery was hard, Elizabeth relished being a mother and was often photographed coddling her new baby. When a reporter asked what her favorite scent was, she quickly replied, "Babies and bacon."

With a new marriage and a new baby, Elizabeth seemed ready to devote herself to the role of wife and mother and even commented that she enjoyed just staying at home contentedly reading while Michael, Sr., smoked his pipe. But financial strain soon caused the first cracks in the marriage. After they married, Elizabeth arranged for MGM to give Wilding a contract, but the studio was hard pressed to find him decent roles. After receiving a variety of embarrassing scripts, Wilding began declining offers. Much to Elizabeth's dismay, they had to borrow money from MGM to buy their very modern home up in the Hollywood hills. On Elizabeth's twenty-third birthday, her second son, Christopher, was born. It was another difficult cesarean section and her recuperation period was so long that MGM put her on suspension.

By now the Wilding marriage was in serious trouble. Michael—the most popular star in Britain—was basically out of work and his seemingly untroubled attitude grated on Elizabeth's nerves. Montgomery Clift served as the couple's mediator at one point and Elizabeth began to seek comfort in food. She craved

OPPOSITE *Elizabeth settled naturally into her new role as wife and mother. Her second son, Christopher, was born on her twenty-third birthday.*

Elizabeth visits Wilding on the set and shares a laugh with her former co-star Robert Taylor. Things at home were not as amicable. Wilding was not satisfied with the roles MGM offered him and as money grew tighter and tempers flared, the fighting and drinking began.

excitement but felt she was living the life of a middle-aged woman. It was in this state that Taylor met Mike Todd, the brash forty-nine-year-old producer, show-man, entrepreneur, and personality extraordinaire. Todd made his intentions clear to Taylor: he wanted to marry her. She was exhilarated by his bravado and his magnetism. A day after she announced her separation from Wilding, Todd grabbed Taylor by the hand, pushed her into a chair and declared he was going to marry her and left no room for her to dissent. There was no risk of that, however, for Elizabeth was enthralled and dazzled by this man who could take complete control of her.

Mike Todd directing a scene on the set of Around the World in 80 Days, *which won the Oscar for best picture. At the ceremony, Elizabeth stood by his side as he gushed that he was the luckiest man alive and joked, "I don't know if I can live through all this!"*

Elizabeth's image had changed dramatically during her marriage to Mike Todd. More than ever, she played the part of the movie queen to the hilt, and was often photographed dripping in jewels and furs.

The two had a whirlwind courtship and Todd—who once boasted of winning and losing a million dollars by the time he was nineteen—lavished an appreciative Taylor with gaudy jewels, furs, and paintings. On February 2, 1957, Taylor and Todd were married in Mexico. Todd's best friend, singer Eddie Fisher, served as best man and Fisher's wife, MGM musical darling Debbie Reynolds, was matron of honor. The Todds' Acapulco honeymoon was interrupted by Taylor's extreme back pain, the result of spinal surgery she had undergone a few

Todd was the proverbial tough guy with a soft touch. He and Elizabeth's boys were mutually devoted to each other. As always, Elizabeth managed to fit some quiet family time into her whirlwind life with Todd.

months earlier after slipping on a yacht and landing flat on her back. With Todd hovering protectively over her, Taylor was flown to New York, where doctors discovered that Taylor was not only suffering from serious spinal damage, but she was also a few months pregnant.

Elizabeth's ailments and pregnancy didn't stop the couple from embarking that year on a city-to-city tour promoting Todd's ambitious film *Around the World in 80 Days* (1956). During her time with Todd, Elizabeth changed drastically. She seemed to live by Todd's motto, "Audacity makes the star," and as a star, she felt entitled to the lavish lifestyle he provided for her. She was whisked off in Todd's private plane, dined on champagne and caviar, was chauffeured in a Rolls-Royce, and was attired in diamonds and furs. When Todd won the 1957 Academy Award for his production of *Around the World in 80 Days*, Elizabeth—sporting a new diamond tiara—stood by his side beaming. But the Todds were also well-known brawlers and would often resort to public wrestling and screaming matches. They fought hard and loved hard. Elizabeth later admitted she wanted a strong man who could control her and admitted loving how Mike would lose his temper and dominate her.

In August 1957 the Todds had a daughter, Liza, whom Elizabeth delivered prematurely by cesarean section. Shortly afterward, Elizabeth began filming *Cat on a Hot Tin Roof* (1958), with her husband's enthusiastic approval. Seven months into the shooting, Mike Todd was to attend an event in his honor in New York. Elizabeth had planned to be with him, but a last-minute virus kept her home in bed. Todd's private plane, *The Liz*, headed out that stormy March night. After hitting a wall of fog over New Mexico, the plane plummeted to the ground, killing all aboard. In her autobiography, Debbie Reynolds described a hysterical Elizabeth running down the stairs in her nightgown after being told the tragic news and heading for the front door before collapsing and being carried back to her room. There she remained, in a sedated stupor, until Todd's funeral, held in his hometown of Chicago.

Eddie Fisher was just as devastated over Mike's death as Elizabeth. Reynolds, who had two children of her own with Fisher, took in Taylor's three kids for a while and sent Eddie over to comfort Elizabeth. Soon it was catching the media's attention that the two were spending an inordinate amount of time together. Elizabeth later said she could not sleep at the time and would wash down sleeping pills with liquor, which she drank most of the night while reminiscing about Mike with Eddie. Pretty soon, however, their long grief counseling sessions turned into something more.

Elizabeth, overcome with grief and sedated, was supported by both her doctor (left) and brother, Howard (right), during the emotional funeral service for Todd in his hometown of Chicago in 1958.

Although Eddie and Debbie had been on the brink of divorce for a while, the sense of betrayal over his affair with Taylor ran deep. When the rumors first started to circulate about the affair, however, Reynolds feigned ignorance. A newsreel shot at the height of the Reynolds-Fisher-Taylor maelstrom features a smiling Reynolds getting off a plane holding her daughter Carrie and claiming to know nothing, then deftly dropping the subject by having Carrie wave "bye-bye" to the reporters.

Reynolds later wrote that she finally called Eddie—at two in the morning—at his hotel room in the Catskills where he was performing. When he didn't answer, she slyly tried locating him by putting in a call to Elizabeth Taylor's room, telling the operator his pal Dean Martin was on the line. When

A Hollywood Love Triangle

The tragic news of Mike Todd's sudden and violent death just months after the birth of his and Elizabeth's daughter, Liza, shocked the nation. Headlines describing Elizabeth's devastation and pictures of the couple in happier times were splashed across newspapers everywhere. The fact that Todd's best friend, Eddie Fisher, shared Taylor's inconsolable grief was also widely known. The papers also reported that Fisher's wife, MGM musical star Debbie Reynolds, took Taylor's children into her own home after the tragedy and sent her husband to console Elizabeth. Further headlines about the twenty-six-year-old widow wailing between bouts of semiconscious sedation and threatening to throw herself into Todd's open grave only heightened public sympathy for her.

When word started going around that the Widow Todd was spending too much time with Eddie Fisher, though, the public grew suspicious. Reynolds initially ignored these reports, claiming they were merely leaning on each other for support during this terrible time. Gossip mongers bit their tongues as pictures of a bejeweled and radiant Taylor surfaced at a Catskill resort where Fisher was headlining. Public sentiment shifted, bordering on outrage. Gossip columnist Hedda Hopper, a long-time Taylor ally, decided to break the ice and ask Taylor about the Fisher rumors. When an emotional Elizabeth blurted out, "What do you expect me to do, sleep alone?" an indignant Hopper promptly wrote a scathing commentary about Taylor's conduct.

The tabloids had a field day with the Taylor-Fisher-Reynolds love triangle, making it one of the most talked about scandals of the fifties, and Taylor the epitome of the home wrecking femme fatale.

The Fishers accompanied Elizabeth to her first public appearance after Mike's death. Here the cameras capture Eddie getting quite an eyeful of Elizabeth.

Overnight, Taylor and Fisher were vilified and public sympathy swung into the corner of the scorned Reynolds, America's musical sweetheart. Everywhere Taylor and Fisher went they were heckled by crowds and various organizations upholding decency. Even the pope got in on the action by deeming Taylor a lascivious, immoral adulterer. This papal condemnation was widely publicized in the papers, but while it was meant to destroy her career—and many thought it would—the titillated public ate it up. Soon MGM was using their star's notorious image to their advantage by publicizing her upcoming steamy role as the sexually charged Maggie the Cat in *Cat on a Hot Tin Roof*. This would not be the first time Taylor's conduct offscreen would affect her career.

Eddie picked up, he discovered it was Debbie, not Dino, and the cat was out of the bag. After a few indignant denials, he finally admitted he and Elizabeth were deeply in love. A few years after this climactic call, Reynolds acknowledged, "I knew it would be someone, but I didn't think it would be Elizabeth."

Before the Fisher-Reynolds divorce became final, "Liz and Eddie" conducted their affair openly and defiantly, causing public jeers and even death threats. In this tumultuous period of involuntary exile the maligned couple became all the more dependent on each other. By the time Elizabeth crossed the

Knowing how chummy the Todds and Fishers were before Mike's untimely death made Elizabeth's liaison and subsequent marriage to Eddie Fisher hard for the public to accept — or forgive.

By the time of Elizabeth's marriage to Fisher in 1959 she had converted to Judaism—more in honor of Mike Todd's memory than for Eddie's sake.

Atlantic to film 1959's *Suddenly, Last Summer,* she was Mrs. Eddie Fisher and had converted to Judaism. But the affair had ruined her chances of winning an Oscar for her Academy Award–nominated performances in *Cat on a Hot Tin Roof* and *Suddenly, Last Summer.*

What made matters worse, however, was the fact that Elizabeth was already feeling uneasy about her latest nuptials. Both Elizabeth and Eddie were clinging to the memory of Mike Todd. Elizabeth went so far as to continue wearing Mike's twisted wedding band, which had been salvaged from the charred plane wreckage. Meanwhile, Eddie tried his best to emulate his former idol—smoking cigars, buying fancy gifts, and tipping lavishly—but he was no match for his late friend and was certainly not the domineering alpha-male Elizabeth craved.

Though still a newlywed, Elizabeth confided to *Suddenly, Last Summer* and *Cleopatra* director Joseph Mankiewicz that her marriage to Eddie was "clearly a mistake" and further conceded that she had tried to keep Mike's memory alive through Eddie, "but I only have his ghost." As for Eddie, he later wrote that he

OPPOSITE *Behind the romantic poses and smiles, Elizabeth's marriage to Eddie was shaky. Elizabeth later told a friend she knew she had made a mistake within seconds of signing their marriage certificate.*

was "obsessed" with Elizabeth but was not prepared for becoming part of her frenetic entourage and gaining recognition as Mr. Elizabeth Taylor. Since their illicit affair, his career had taken a steep nosedive and he was becoming increasingly restless, following Elizabeth from one luxurious hotel suite to another as she worked on location. To pass the time, Eddie drank, lost wads of money playing cards, and continued getting regular "vitamin" boosts from the mysterious syringe of Max Jacobson (a.k.a. Dr. Feelgood). This controversial elixir was nothing more than shots of amphetamines, or speed. At the time, amphetamine usage was controversial but not yet illegal since its insidious addictive nature had not yet been determined. Dr. Feelgood had a long list of famous clients and Fisher later admitted he was Jacobson's "best disciple."

By the time they arrived in Rome, where the filming of *Cleopatra* had been relocated, the relationship had deteriorated significantly. Elizabeth was prone to cruelly snapping at her husband in public. During their stay in Rome, however, Elizabeth decided to adopt a baby with Fisher—no doubt in an effort to try to salvage their disintegrating union. The infant, later named Maria, was German-born and, it turned out, had a deformed hip and was very malnourished. Elizabeth, already known for her soft spot for needy causes, went ahead with the initial legal steps for adoption and began calling the best clinics in Germany to arrange for corrective surgery.

Her recent bout with pneumonia had caused the production of *Cleopatra* to come to a halt and prompted the replacement of two of the main stars: Peter Finch's Caesar was replaced by Rex Harrison, and Stephen Boyd's Marc Antony was now to be played by the Welsh acting dynamo Richard Burton. The latter arrived in Rome with his wife, Sybil, and their two daughters. Gossip columnists were already predicting a love affair between Richard and Elizabeth, since Burton was widely known as a lothario with leading ladies. Burton was also hailed as one of the most talented stage actors to grace the screen since Laurence Olivier. A verbose, hard-drinking, devastatingly witty man of enormous intellect, Burton was certainly a force to be reckoned with. But as the media buzzed about his pending working relationship with Elizabeth Taylor, Richard opined, "All this stuff about Elizabeth being the most beautiful woman in the world is absolute nonsense. She's a pretty girl, of course, and she has wonderful eyes. But she has a double chin and an overdeveloped chest, and she's rather short in the leg."

A photo published of Elizabeth reclining amiably on Eddie's lap on the *Cleopatra* set with a rather bored-looking Richard looking on would seem to

Elizabeth fusses over Richard as her son looks on. Although Burton joked that she only visited his sets to keep a vigilant eye on him, the renowned stage actor credited Elizabeth with giving him invaluable advice on acting before the camera.

corroborate Richard's flippant remarks. But this innocuous photograph soon became notorious worldwide as the attraction between the two stars, which had been simmering on the set since their first scene together, came to a rolling boil. Other photographs began to circulate, such as those of Taylor and Burton sunning themselves and kissing on a yacht. Their respective spouses left Rome in disgust. Sybil Burton, no stranger to Richard's dalliances, was giving Richard time to come back, as he always did. Eddie, however, was completely distraught and on the verge of a nervous breakdown.

With the famed paparazzi of Rome on their heels, "Dick and Liz" were soon on the covers of international papers everywhere. Their adulterous affair knocked Kruschev out of the headlines for weeks, prompting Richard to dub this time in their lives "Le Scandale." Elizabeth's earlier role as the other woman was nothing compared to this. Once again she was condemned as a wanton woman, a shameless home wrecker. And once again she didn't care about the public's outrage, because she was desperately in love with Richard. For his part, Burton was torn between loyalty to his family and his complete fascination with Elizabeth. He nicknamed her Ocean because to him, she was boundless. After two more years of "Le Scandale" and Richard's tortured guilt over his wife, Richard and Elizabeth finally divorced their respective spouses and became husband and wife in Montreal in 1964.

Together, Burton and Taylor became a lucrative cinematic enterprise. The first hints of this came after the release of *Cleopatra*. The film was panned mercilessly by the critics but the box-office receipts soared because the public wanted to see these infamous lovers together on the screen. Meanwhile, Richard was adapting

BELOW *Elizabeth and Richard pose at their Puerto Vallarta home, Casa Kimberly, shortly before their marriage. Their presence in Mexico during the height of their affair and in the years after their marriage transformed the onetime small fishing village into a popular resort.*

OPPOSITE *Although their romance was no longer illicit after their marriage in 1964, the public could still not get enough of the Burtons. Richard proudly marveled over how people would burst into applause or gasp in admiration whenever they saw "my girl."*

well to Elizabeth's children and menagerie. He even formally adopted the little German girl, who was named Maria Burton. But as with Mike Todd, Elizabeth and her new spouse indulged in ostentatious displays and notorious brawls. Their destructive lifestyle, filled with extraordinary amounts of alcohol (see Chapter 4), eventually prevented them from attaining marital bliss.

After twelve tumultuous years together, they divorced in 1974—only to be remarried in 1975. But within months of their second marriage, which Burton claimed was "doomed from the start," they separated and their final divorce was decreed in 1976. As much as they still loved and depended on each other, they realized they had to go their separate ways. Elizabeth aptly told reporters, "I love Richard Burton with every fiber of my soul but we can't be together. We're too

Elizabeth gained self-confidence as a woman with Richard. She told a friend she used to think she was "just a broad," but with him, she felt treated as an equal. On the other hand, she joked about having several gray hairs and naming each strand "Burton."

The Burtons studying their lines for Who's Afraid of Virginia Woolf? *Richard often referred to Elizabeth as "Snapshot" or "Quicktake" because of her great ability to memorize lines in one sitting.*

mutually self-destructive." After more than a decade of decadent living and months in the arms of unlikely suitors, Elizabeth craved the quiet life.

She saw her chance at domestic bliss in the form of John Warner, a wealthy Virginia politician who had ambitions for a seat in the United States Senate. They met in Washington, D.C., where Warner was chairing the Bicentennial administration. Recently divorced from heiress Catherine Mellon, Warner was considered a good catch—tall, ruggedly handsome, and very comfortable financially. After a brief courtship, Warner presented Taylor with an engagement ring of patriotic red, white, and blue gems.

Elizabeth made the usual proclamations of love and told the world that all she wanted to do was to live her life on the farm as Mrs. John Warner. Unfortunately, Elizabeth got what she asked for. After relentless campaigning, Warner was elected to office in 1979, no doubt partly due to Elizabeth's popularity and presence at countless campaign barbecues. After his election, Senator Warner promptly left "his little heifer" on the farm to attend to business in Washington, D.C. The marriage was soon obviously on the rocks and when she wasn't out partying at Studio 54 (see chapter 5), Elizabeth languished on the farm, lying alone in bed, watching television while eating and drinking her troubles away. It was during this dark time that Elizabeth ballooned to a staggering 190 pounds (85 kg) and became the butt of fat jokes.

In 1980 Elizabeth slimmed down at the prospect of a professional comeback. This time it would be her stage debut, in *The Little Foxes*. At first Warner gushed with farmboy pride over his wife being the star of the show, but much to his chagrin, the play was a Broadway hit and his wife's professional ambitions reawakened under the footlights. After years out of the spotlight, Elizabeth obviously felt quite at home. She was in her element once again and was not about to give it up. In a telling moment before the cameras, Elizabeth was asked if she was planning to work more in the flush of this successful comeback. Warner, who stood beside her, semiseriously barked out a firm "No!" and began to guide her out of camera range before Elizabeth could reply. While Elizabeth cackled a bit sarcastically, she quickly turned to the reporter and said in a perfectly timed conspiratorial tone, "We'll talk later."

Elizabeth solemnly walks out of a 1984 London memorial service for Richard Burton, 58, who died of a cerebral hemorrhage at his home in Céligny, Switzerland. Although they both had known that reconciliation was impossible, they still loved each other deeply and spoke on the phone almost daily up until the time of his death.

By late 1981 the Warners had separated. While touring in Los Angeles, Elizabeth was hospitalized for chest pains and spent much of her recovery time speaking on the phone with the recently separated Richard Burton, who soon escorted Taylor to her fiftieth birthday bash. Although the press gleefully suspected yet another reconciliation, Burton quelled these rumors by stating, "The best way for Elizabeth and myself to keep each other together is to be apart." They raised hopes again in 1983 by starring together on Broadway as a dueling couple in Noel Coward's *Private Lives,* but during the run Richard married again and Elizabeth promptly announced a short-lived engagement to Victor Luna, a doting, wealthy Mexican lawyer. When Burton died suddenly of a cerebral hemorrhage the following year, Elizabeth was devastated. Burton's widow later opined, "Elizabeth can't face up to the fact that when you've lost someone twice, you really have lost them—and she did."

Although she "almost made a mistake" by planning to marry New York businessman Dennis Stein in the mid-eighties, it wasn't until 1991 that Elizabeth walked down the aisle again—this time with a rugged blonde construction worker twenty years her junior. Elizabeth and Larry Fortensky met as patients at the Betty Ford Center. The brawny, quiet type, Fortensky seemed conspicuously out of place during the circuslike atmosphere of their wedding at Michael Jackson's surreal Neverland ranch in California's Santa Ynez Valley. During her sixtieth birthday bash, held at Disneyland, Fortensky stood by his glamorous bride like a bodyguard, blinking at the ceaseless firing of camera bulbs.

For a while Fortensky tried to maintain his identity and even packed his own lunch and nobly headed out to the construction site every morning. For her part, Taylor tried to ease Fortensky into her entourage-filled existence and even had a basketball court and bachelor's quarters installed in her Bel-Air mansion where Larry could enjoy a casual retreat. But after two hip surgeries in 1995, Elizabeth endured a long and hard convalescence that caused irreparable damage to her eighth marriage. By early 1996 Elizabeth filed for divorce, and three years later swore shrilly during a Barbara Walters interview that she would never marry again. But the rumors persist, especially since Taylor has become chummy with actor Rod Steiger. Both actors maintain, however, that their close relationship is strictly platonic.

A slim and tan Taylor holds hands with Larry Fortensky, the construction worker she met while both were patients at the Betty Ford Center. Fortensky, twenty years Taylor's junior, became husband number eight in 1991.

CHAPTER FOUR

Diva

Elizabeth's bombastic lifestyle was launched after landing the unprecedented million-dollar contract to star in *Cleopatra* and her subsequent partnership (both on- and offscreen) with Richard Burton. Although she had certainly tasted the good life before—especially during her time with Mike Todd—Elizabeth reached new heights of indulgence in the sixties with Burton. Ironically, her initial request for the million-dollar salary to portray Cleopatra was meant as a joke. Eddie and Elizabeth were in Paris when her agent phoned with news that the producers of *Cleopatra* wanted her to star in the film. Flippantly, she told her agent (through Eddie) that she'd do it for a million dollars, assuming the producers would reject her terms. Her plan—no doubt to her later delight—backfired. Not only was she guaranteed a cool million as the Queen of the Nile, but she also received perks

PAGE 76 *Elizabeth and Richard making quite an entrance at a charity costume ball in Italy. The Burtons' flamboyant lifestyle—which made headlines all over the world—soon became the template for 1960s jetsetters.*

PAGE 77 *Andy Warhol's 1964 lithograph print of "Liz" secured Taylor's status in pop culture, along with Marilyn Monroe, Jacqueline Kennedy, and the Campbell's soup can. Years later, Warhol partied with Elizabeth at New York's glitzy Studio 54.*

unheard of for an actor at that time, including 10 percent of the film's gross box-office sales and $3,000 per week for living expenses, food, and lodging. By the time the beleaguered, overschedule production wrapped, Elizabeth walked away with more than $7 million.

Elizabeth's lifestyle in London and eventually Rome, where the film relocated after her near fatal bout with pneumonia, was indeed worthy of a queen. Elizabeth, Eddie, and her three children (whom she always wanted near her) were flown to each location first class, situated at the Dorchester in London and later in an opulent fourteen-room Roman villa bustling with secretaries, nannies, servants, dogs, and cats. Over this seeming chaos, Elizabeth coolly presided, her every whim met with instant gratification. If she so fancied, her favorite chili

ABOVE *Elizabeth was already living like a queen when she met Burton. Many people, Elizabeth included, teased Burton that he just latched onto the million-dollar star to increase his own wealth and fame.*

LEFT *The Burtons' escalating wealth and their incessant flaunting of their riches gave rise to several critical attacks in the press. In response to being called ostentatious and vulgar, Elizabeth, shown here in Cleopatra, laughed, "would you want me any other way?"*

BELOW *Even Taylor's detractors couldn't deny her sultry appeal. Burton devoted numerous passages in his diaries to his steadfast awe over her beauty.*

would arrive from Chasen's in L.A.; succulent stone crabs would be sent from the coast of Florida; sirloin steaks would arrive straight out of Chicago; shrimp Creole would be shipped from New Orleans; and smoked salmon would be flown in from New York.

When Elizabeth and Richard Burton got together, this luxurious lifestyle escalated. Both actors were drawing huge salaries, negotiating lucrative film percentages, and funneling their millions into bank accounts in Switzerland, where they had a home, and into trust funds for the children. Richard, the product of a dirt-poor Welsh family from a grimy mining town, enjoyed his wealth to the maximum. In addition to the staggering amount of money spent on jewels, clothing, and extravagant daily living expenses, the Burtons had a fleet of Rolls-Royces; a yacht adorned with original Monet, Utrillo, and Van Gogh paintings; and later, their own jet. Elizabeth subsequently admitted that these were over-the-top days but quickly added that she was glad she had the opportunity to enjoy this glittering, globe-trotting time while she was young.

It must be noted that, with all the trappings of life as a diva, Elizabeth always cherished motherhood. She never attempted to provide her children with a "normal childhood" because she, herself, had never known one. She did, however, make sure she was always there for them—even when they eventually went off to school. If a child was sick she'd fly to his or her side, and she always wanted the family together for holidays. Her intense love for animals never waned either, and she always had various furry and feathered creatures wandering around; at any given time, the household could be thrown into turmoil over a pet's demise. At one point, the Burtons even used their yacht as a kennel of sorts for their dogs when customs prohibited the animals from staying with

In a photo reminiscent of her early MGM days, Elizabeth shares a moment with the elusive sandpiper. To this day, Elizabeth's retains a special affinity for the vulnerable— whether they be animals, children, the sick, or the troubled.

them on land. Richard adapted to this circuslike atmosphere well enough, although his increasing dependence on alcohol could cause him to lash out verbally. Although they proved to be self-destructive in the years to come, both Elizabeth and Richard had their hearts in the right place when it came to other people.

At a certain point, however, even friends were claiming to have trouble getting in touch with the Burtons because of their formidable and overprotective retinue. As with royalty, this caused a disadvantageous isolation from the world, which perhaps led to boredom and booze and a dangerous dependence on each other. The Burtons were even becoming professionally dependent on each other. After *Cleopatra*, the couple made eight films together, almost consecutively. When they weren't working together on a film, their advantageous contracts stipulated that they could not be more than one hour away from each other. This clause could make production costs—and no doubt tempers—soar. In 1968, for

OPPOSITE *Elizabeth's role as Martha in* Who's Afraid of Virginia Woolf? *was the crowning glory of her career. The film, directed by their friend Mike Nichols, won five Academy Awards, including best actress for Elizabeth. Sadly, it marked the peak of her career, for none of her future roles would ever match it.*

instance, the Burtons insisted that both their films be shot in Paris, even though Richard's film was set in London and Elizabeth's film, *The Only Game in Town* (released in 1970), was supposed to be set in Las Vegas! Needless to say, the budget for the latter hit the ceiling since mock casinos had to be constructed.

Of all their films together, only *Who's Afraid of Virginia Woolf?* (1966) was highly praised by critics. *The Taming of the Shrew* (1967) was a close second in terms of inspired performances, but the critics did not embrace the Burtons as tempestuous Shakespearean lovers as much as they did contemporary drunken brawlers. The set of *Who's Afraid of Virginia Woolf?* was emotionally draining for the

ABOVE *Although everyone, including Richard, had reservations about Elizabeth taking on Shakespeare in* The Taming of the Shrew, *Taylor turned in a fine performance. Filming went smoothly and the couple later reflected that their stay in Italy was like a second honeymoon.*

OPPOSITE *Although her overall experience during the production of* The Taming of the Shrew *was positive, it was during filming that Montgomery Clift died suddenly at the age of forty-five, leaving Elizabeth completely grief-stricken.*

Burtons; their performances as a dueling, hard-drinking codependent couple came too close to home. Indeed, during rehearsals, Richard, feeling every bit the hen-pecked husband, sighed, "I *am* George."

Although the two might spend the night drinking, they were always punctual and professional on the set. This was something coworkers have long remarked about Elizabeth in particular. But as the years went by, her many illnesses—including chronic back pain, sciatica, and a partial hysterectomy—would rack up costly delays until producers were soon afraid that they couldn't afford her from an insurance standpoint.

BELOW *By the late 1960s, Elizabeth's increasing dependence on painkillers and alcohol became more of a problem. Elizabeth's use of prescription drugs rose as her health problems increased.*

During the filming of 1968's The Only Game in Town, Elizabeth's father, Francis Taylor, died. Elizabeth was severely depressed over his death and further plagued by a bout of sciatica, and the production was shut down for a week.

In 1970 the Burtons took a sabbatical from filmmaking. Elizabeth's precarious health, her drinking, and her overmedication were putting a great strain on their marriage. In the beginning Elizabeth seemed to join Richard at the bar just to be with him and prove she could be his best drinking buddy. But by this time it was Richard who would go on the wagon for months at a time and try in vain to stop Elizabeth's penchant for liquid lunches. For years Elizabeth's roles had been becoming extensions of her legendary status as an over-the-top, jet-

setting globe-trotter, but never was this phenomenon more apparent than in the embarrassingly campy *X, Y and Zee* (released 1972), perhaps the worst movie Elizabeth ever made. She was criticized for being a parody of herself, with exaggerated makeup and enormous wigs. Costar Michael Caine gushed that Elizabeth "was smashing to work with" but conceded that her fussing entourage "made one think they were working with the Statue of Liberty."

Just before shooting this debacle, Elizabeth mourned the sudden death of her much-loved and relied-upon personal secretary, Dick Hanley, who dated back to the Mike Todd days. At Elizabeth's insistence, Richard stayed with her on the frantic *X, Y and Zee* set until he left to film *Anne of the Thousand Days* (1969). Although she coveted the role of the ill-fated Anne Boleyn, the thirty-nine-year-old Elizabeth was gently told she was "too mature" for the part. Indeed—happily— Elizabeth became a grandmother for the first time in 1971 when eighteen-year-old

During the filming of X, Y and Zee, *Elizabeth was still getting over the death of her beloved personal secretary and battling both Richard and the bottle off the set, yet co-star Michael Caine enthused over Elizabeth's professionalism.*

Michael Wilding and his first wife, Beth, had a baby girl named Leyla. Although Elizabeth bought the young couple a beautiful town house and Jaguar at the time of their marriage, Michael was more intersted in pursuing a counter-culture lifestyle. A sometime musician who later moved to Wales to grow organic food, Michael even went so far as to tell the press that his mother's life was "as fantastic to me as it must be to everyone else" and added, "I just don't dig all those diamonds and things."

With such sentiments, Michael must have looked upon Elizabeth's fortieth birthday bash in Budapest with disgust. Richard, who was filming *Bluebeard* (1972) there, presented Elizabeth with the $50,000 Taj Mahal diamond pendant. Remarkably, he stuck to sipping mineral water during the weekend boozefest. Celebrated friends appeared for the festivities at their ritzy hotel, including Princess Grace of Monaco, Michael Caine, Ringo Starr, and David Niven. But later in the year, a tragedy changed their lives forever. Richard's beloved brother, Ifor, died and Richard plunged into the darkest, most violent alcoholic binge he had ever experienced. He blamed himself for the fact that Ifor had become paralyzed four years earlier in a freak accident at the Burtons' home in Gstaad. Richard's drunkenness led to many violent quarrels with Elizabeth, and finally to adultery. Richard had maintained that up to then, he had been completely faithful to Elizabeth during their eight-year marriage, but once he began dallying with women on the set of *Bluebeard*, he knew "the game was up."

Ironically, in 1973 the two starred in a horrific two-part television drama called *Divorce His/Divorce Hers*. It was their last collaboration on film and the beginning of the end of their own turbulent marriage. Soon after, the Burtons separated and Elizabeth took up with a Dutch-born businessman and Hollywood used-car salesman who had a reputation as a gigolo. But it wasn't long before the

Soon after the announcement of Elizabeth's engagement to John Warner, the couple spends a day with their families in Vienna, Austria. Left to right are Michael Wilding, Jr., Liza Todd, Mary Warner, Elizabeth, John, and Michael's daughter Naomi and wife Jo.

Elizabeth looking every bit the incognito movie star. Everywhere she went, an army of personal assistants, chauffeurs, bodyguards, press secretaries, hair dressers, make-up artists, and dog walkers followed. Although the Burtons treated their retinue as family, by the mid-1970s, the lack of privacy was beginning to wear thin for Richard.

Diamonds Are a Girl's Best Friend

Although Taylor's penchant for jewels was an early trait especially catered to by her third husband, Mike Todd, it wasn't until her lucrative union with Richard Burton that her multimillion dollar jewel collection made national headlines.

Burton presented Elizabeth with a most impressive engagement ring: the 33.19-carat Krupp diamond, which once belonged to the wife of a German steel magnate. Taylor, who had converted to Judaism after Mike Todd's death, joked about the irony of "a Jewish girl" now owning the bulbous bauble once belonging to a rich German woman. Also from Richard, Elizabeth acquired a bracelet once belonging to Empress Josephine Bonaparte, and most notably, a huge pearl that had graced royal necks in both England and Spain. "La Pelegrina" was an enormous pearl pendant given to Queen Mary I ("Bloody Mary") by King Philip II of Spain at the time of their marriage in 1555.

In the 1960s, in additon to countless emeralds, sapphires, and rubies, Burton also presented Taylor with the famous Taj Mahal diamond and purchased one of the world's most perfect diamonds, the unbelievable 62.42-carat Cartier diamond, soon dubbed the Taylor-Burton diamond. Before settling into Taylor's hands, the diamond was displayed for the public to see at Cartier. Later Taylor had the tremendous gem—too large to wear on her hand—transformed into a pendant.

In his journal, Burton recalled once calling out to Taylor, asking what she was doing in the adjacent room. Burton wrote with obvious pleasure that in a childlike voice, she told him that she was playing with her jewels.

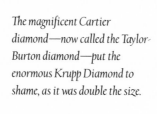

Elizabeth models the Cartier diamond after having it fashioned into a pendant, which hung from an impressive double strand of even more diamonds. When told her enormous baubles were vulgar, Elizabeth answered, "ain't it great?"

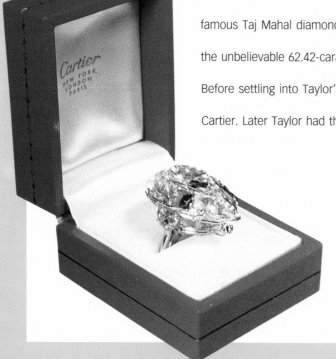

The magnificent Cartier diamond—now called the Taylor-Burton diamond—put the enormous Krupp Diamond to shame, as it was double the size.

During her marriage to Richard Burton, Elizabeth's already impressive jewel collection nearly doubled. "The more, the better has always been my motto," Elizabeth later explained.

Burtons were back together and celebrating their tenth wedding anniversary in California. Yet it was short-lived. The booze was always present and Richard was still succumbing to the charms of other women. Telling friends she could do no more for him, Elizabeth left again. This was the pattern the two blindly followed for the next few years—leading them to divorce, a brief remarriage, and another divorce. Theirs was ultimately a sad love story that did not end until Richard was buried in 1984.

BELOW *By the mid-eighties, Elizabeth was more or less famous for being Elizabeth Taylor. She used this fame not only to further humanitarian causes, but to launch a lucrative perfume business.*

ABOVE *After years out of the limelight as Mrs. John Warner, Elizabeth made a successful comeback on Broadway, instigating a brief re-entry into film with a part in Agatha Christie's* The Mirror Crack'd.

In the late seventies and early eighties, Elizabeth reached an all-time low. With her marriage to Senator John Warner languishing, Elizabeth became more entrenched in the dangerous cycle of drinking and taking painkillers. Bored after so much time spent alone on the farm, Elizabeth then burst out onto the sybaritic Studio 54 scene. With her friend, the designer Halston, at her side, Elizabeth presided over the trendy scene with the likes of Andy Warhol, Liza Minelli, and Mick Jagger, and spent many dizzying nights under the disco ball. Elizabeth's extravagant lifestyle had finally eclipsed her reputation as an Academy Award–winning actress.

While she did make a professional comeback with a Broadway hit and starred in a few made-for-television films, her personal life was in a shambles. She later admitted to being hooked on Percodan, a potent postoperative painkiller. Friends at this time were alarmed by her spacey appearance and demeanor. After a steady month of drinking and drug binges in 1983, Elizabeth collapsed and was hospitalized. While there, her concerned family and friends, including Roddy McDowall, joined together and begged Elizabeth to seek professional help for her addiction. She listened in shocked silence and later recalled that she "couldn't believe what I had become." A few days later, Elizabeth Taylor became the first celebrity to check into the Betty Ford Center, a drug and alcohol rehabilitation clinic located in the California desert. It was the start of a new life.

Since her enormous weight gain in the late seventies, Elizabeth has struggled to control her weight. That her favorite food is southern fried chicken with all the trimmings doesn't help matters.

MIRAMAX FILMS
RELAIS & CHATEAUX
CINEMA
AGAINST AIDS
Moulin de Mougins
SPONSORS
CHOPARD
MIRAMAX FILMS

CHAPTER FIVE

Mother Courage

$\mathcal{I}$n this day and age of tell-all tabloid TV, it seems hard to believe that Taylor's act of openly checking herself into a rehab clinic could cause the stir that it did. Suddenly, other addicted stars—including her old friend Peter Lawford—had the courage to seek treatment. Her action put the Betty Ford Center on the map. While there, Elizabeth not only suffered from withdrawal symptoms, but was shocked to discover that she had a roommate and was required to wash her own clothes and mop the floors—things to which she was not accustomed. She emerged a bit shaky, but noticeably stronger, both physically and mentally.

In 1985 Elizabeth set yet another precedent. She was the first person to publicly denounce the homophobic stigma associated with AIDS. Her old friend Rock Hudson had recently succumbed to the disease after months of

PAGE 94 *As hostess at the annual Cinema Against AIDS in Cannes in 1999, Elizabeth had to ad-lib, reading her notes with a penlight when a blackout struck just as she was announced. When the lights came back up, Elizabeth hollered with delight and the crowd burst into applause.*

PAGE 95 *Elizabeth's story has sold countless publications, since her own life—filled with romance, wealth, tragedy, and brushes with death—has proven to be more dramatic than any film role.*

LEFT *Magic Johnson (left), who announced he was HIV-positive in the early 1990s, towers over Elizabeth at Macy's Passport 1996 AIDS fund-raiser. Michael Johnson, 1996 Olympic winner, is on the right.*

cagey denial of having the virus. Elizabeth was devastated by his death and outraged over the public's tendency to treat people with AIDS like untouchables. Although she was advised not to speak out on such a controversial subject, Elizabeth could not be stopped, and she energetically spearheaded a crusade to educate the public about the disease and to help raise money for research.

Taylor's cause became all the more passionate when Aileen Getty, the former wife of her son Christopher and the mother of his two children, tested positive for HIV, as did Elizabeth's secretary and good friend, Roger Wall, who later committed suicide in 1991 because he had AIDS. Aileen Getty later said that

Passion and Compassion

Elizabeth was particularly aghast at Hollywood's initial timidity about the subject of homosexuality and AIDS, because as she pointed out, so many of their brightest talents were gay.

When news of a spreading disease that ravaged the immune system was first being reported in the early 1980s, not many people—including then-President Ronald Reagan—spoke of it. This devastating viral infection, called auto-immune deficiency syndrome (AIDS), was initially considered a gay man's disease, since the first major outbreaks were in urban, gay communities in San Francisco and New York. Many Christian organizations even felt that AIDS was an expression of the wrath of God, punishing homosexuals for their sinful lifestyles. Ignorance and bias combined to produce a powerful stigma associated with the disease.

The first publicly acknowledged AIDS-related death to shock Hollywood came in the mid-eighties when Rock Hudson, Elizabeth's former costar and dear friend succumbed to it. By now the nation's death toll was rising and although research had shown that the disease was spread through blood contact—including tainted blood transfusions—the stigma of AIDS remained. Deeply affected by Hudson's death, Taylor began to speak out about AIDS, against the wishes of both her friends and her professional advisors. The fact that many of her dearest friends—and, in fact, many within the talented Hollywood community—were gay served to fuel Taylor's fire. She soon formed the American Foundation for AIDS Research (AmFAR) and spoke out before Congress, seeking better funding for research.

Elizabeth has often said about her AIDS activism that she is finally using her public image in a positive way. Indeed, she has used her prominent stature in the press to publicize the call for humanity and understanding for people with AIDS. Her support and personal appearances have reaped millions of dollars in the name of AIDS research. In a recent interview, Taylor said she would be perfectly happy traveling the rest of her days seeking support and funding for all her "kids" with AIDS.

Although her days as a highly paid working actress are largely over, Elizabeth has accepted her role as a Hollywood institution with regal grace.

she didn't know what would have become of her if her former mother-in-law had not taken her in and ensured that she had the best medical care. Elizabeth was soon the first witness to testify before Congress about funding for the National Institute of Health, and she cofounded the American Foundation for AIDS Research (AmFAR).

Elizabeth had already garnered a reputation as a Hollywood legend and stalwart survivor. Now she was being lauded as a humanitarian. It's easy for detractors to claim that her efforts were prompted by a desire for personal publicity, but Elizabeth's long track record of empathy toward the suffering belies such accusations. That's not to say Elizabeth did not retain her taste for the good life. She enjoyed close friendships with other highly visible celebs, including

Elizabeth poses with New York City schoolchildren after talking to them about AIDS in 1993. Elizabeth surprised many with her tenacity in support of AIDS research and awareness—and she's proved to be a rather formidable advocate.

Michael Jackson—who shared with her an unconventional childhood marked by early fame—and Malcolm Forbes, the late multimillionaire and publisher. Together, Taylor and Forbes hosted his extravagant seventieth birthday party in Morocco. Taylor was seen wearing various pricey baubles from Forbes and photographers snapped her on the back of his Harley-Davidson motorcycle. The press began to wonder if this would be marriage number eight. This was denied by both parties and, after Forbes's death, reports of his homosexuality surfaced.

Another milestone was reached in 1987 with the debut of Elizabeth Taylor's "Passion," a violet-scented, upscale perfume she helped create. During the promo-

After the phenomenal success of *"Passion,"* the slim and elegant star unveiled a new, high-end scent called *"White Diamonds."* Elizabeth had begun a new and lucrative career in the perfume business.

Elizabeth's ill-health has led to costly delays in filming since her days as a child star; during Cleopatra, *she nearly died of pneumonia.*

tional campaign, Elizabeth made various appearances at department stores, in boutiques, and in television commercials, where, swathed in purple and sparkling with diamonds, she told viewers, "I have a passion for life." This oft-repeated quote soon became the mantra of the "Passion" line, which proved to be a phenomenal success, grossing an estimated $70 million in a year. Taylor easily recouped all the money she had lost since her multimillion dollar days as a topnotch actress. It wasn't long before she helped "Unlock the Mystery" by unveiling yet another successful perfume, "White Diamonds."

The following year, Elizabeth succumbed once more to alcohol and drug abuse. She flew back to the desert and checked herself into the Betty Ford Center.

Even with a neck brace, Elizabeth manages a dazzling smile. Over the years, Elizabeth's various illnesses and her accident proneness have become a part of her legend. Even second husband Michael Wilding once joked, "Elizabeth is allergic to good health."

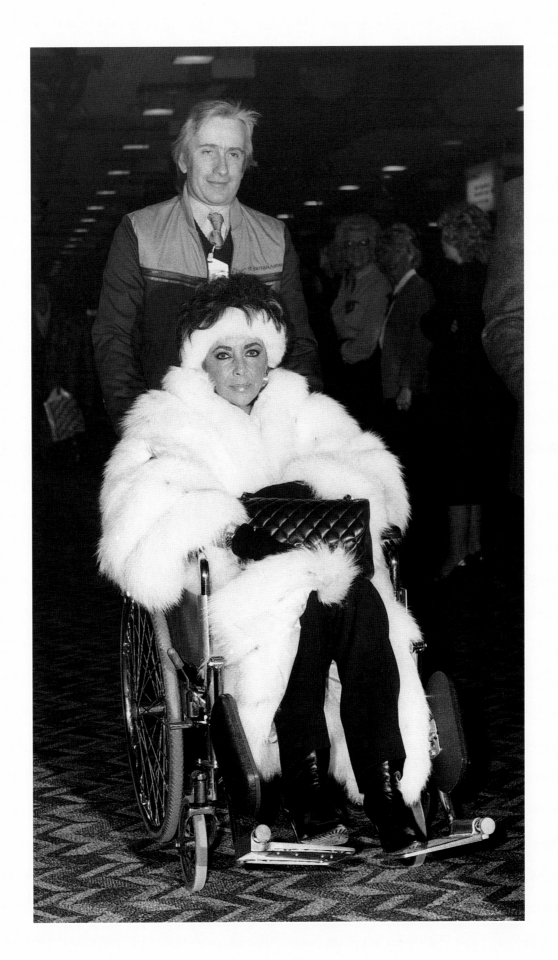

Elizabeth being wheeled out of an airport in the mid-1980s after twisting her ankle while on a trip with former paramour George Hamilton.

This stay was a bit different from her original stint. Because of her chronic back problems, Elizabeth was excused from various exercises and had to be pushed around in a wheelchair. One of the most circulated shots in the tabloids at the time was that of Elizabeth being pushed in her wheelchair by a fellow patient—a strapping, much younger Larry Fortensky. For a year after their Betty Ford Center stay, Elizabeth and Larry remained friends and provided each other with much-needed support. As she had done in 1983, Elizabeth held Alcoholics Anonymous meetings at her home, which were attended by former Betty Ford patients, including Fortensky. Thus began their relationship, which went from a platonic, supportive friendship to that of husband and wife.

Sober again, Elizabeth threw herself back into her AIDS work, helping to raise millions for the cause while keeping up a rigorous schedule promoting her lucrative fragrance enterprise. Her friendships with the likes of Malcolm Forbes, Saudi Arms dealer Adnan Khashoggi, and Michael Jackson boosted AmFAR's coffers, as Elizabeth requested that each of her high-powered friends donate a million dollars for AIDS research. In return, Elizabeth's friends could expect her loyalty—especially in times of trouble. When Khashoggi was under house arrest for allegedly helping the late Philippine president Ferdinand Marcos funnel millions out of the Philippine treasury, Elizabeth turned up at Khashoggi's party in New York. And when Michael Jackson was accused of molesting a young boy, Elizabeth flew to the aid of her friend and maintained to the public her steadfast support.

After years of appearing in mediocre, made-for-television movies, Elizabeth returned to the big screen in 1994 in a cameo appearance as Fred Flintstone's nagging mother-in-law in Steven Spielberg's movie version of *The Flintstones* (1994). It was not exactly a role worthy of an Academy Award–winning actress, but it was an obvious bit of camp that Elizabeth seemed to enjoy. Her contract stipulated that proceeds from the film's benefit premiere were to be donated to the Elizabeth Taylor AIDS Foundation, which she founded after becoming disappointed with AmFAR management.

That same year, in September, Sara Sothern Taylor died at the ripe old age of ninety-nine. Elizabeth had long since reconciled with her mother, with whom she had had a turbulent relationship. But Sara never let go of the gilded image of her famous daughter. In Sara's golden years, Elizabeth made arrangements for her mother to live in comfort (with caregivers next door) at a condominium in Rancho Mirage, California, where she remained active, playing bridge and getting around on an oversized tricycle. Upon her mother's death, Taylor made arrangements for Sara to be buried next to Francis, who had died of a stroke in 1968.

OPPOSITE *Although Elizabeth and her mother had periods of great conflict and estrangement, Sara lived to be ninety-nine years old—giving the mother and daughter plenty of time to smooth over their differences. Indeed, Elizabeth remained the apple of Sara's eye until the day Sara died.*

After taping a successful voice-over for The Simpsons, *Elizabeth once again stepped on a soundstage—this time, in an uproariously hammy cameo as Fred Flintstone's glamorous, nagging mother-in-law in Steven Spielberg's* The Flintstones.

Elizabeth's health, never robust, continued to deteriorate. In 1995 she had both hips replaced and then required more surgery because one leg was shorter than the other. It was a long, painful convalescence that caused irreparable damage to her marriage with Fortensky. By early 1996 Elizabeth had filed for divorce. Her lawyers then battled with Fortensky over his exorbitant monetary requests. A free woman once again, Elizabeth continued devoting most of her time to various AIDS events, including the National AIDS Quilt Names Project in Washington, D.C. Back in action, Taylor made cameo appearances on all four of the CBS network's Monday night television comedies, including *The Nanny*, during sweeps week.

But then in early 1997, just weeks before her sixty-fifth birthday, doctors discovered she had a benign brain tumor. In an interview, Taylor said the first symptoms appeared while she was in her bedroom and she suddenly heard herself screaming and babbling. Her son Michael, who lives outside L.A., happened to be visiting and promptly called her doctor. When the doctor did arrive, he at first thought Taylor had been drinking again. When it was obvious that she hadn't, she was taken to the hospital, where it was determined that she had experienced a seizure.

Brain surgery no doubt ranks as the most fearsome of operations, but in typical fashion, Taylor faced this next health crisis with unflinching courage. She even postponed the delicate surgery until after a previously arranged Los Angeles AIDS benefit celebrating her birthday took place. This star-studded, televised event at the Pantages Theater was a tribute to Taylor, who sat in the front row bejeweled and beaming as former Hollywood stars of her day and current celebrities, including Madonna, paid gushing homage to "La Liz." Michael Jackson, who had recently named Taylor godmother of his first child, was there and performed a song he wrote for her, entitled, "Elizabeth." The event raised more than a million dollars for the Elizabeth Taylor AIDS Foundation. A few days later, doctors successfully removed a golfball-sized tumor located behind her left ear that had been pressing against her brain.

Taylor admitted in a *Life* magazine article that before the surgery, she was terrified something terrible might happen—the knife might slip and she might become a vegetable. On the eve of the surgery, she wrote that if she were to die, she and her family, who had gathered around her, could at least take comfort in the fact that she had lived an extraordinary life. But Elizabeth was not ready to die and recovered remarkably well after the four-hour operation. In fact, after the surgery, Elizabeth said she experienced "wild joy" upon regaining her unaltered consciousness. She was, however, bald, and sported a glaring seven-inch (17.5 cm) scar stretching from her left ear to the crown of her head.

In a television interview, Taylor said she immediately asked to see a mirror, but rather than bemoan her scary appearance, she instead wanted to inspect the back of her head because she always wanted to know if she had a flat "pillow head" or a "nice round head." To her delight, she discovered her head was round. When asked how she could laugh at such a time, Elizabeth soberly exclaimed, "What else are you going to do?" She has since been taking medication to control seizures and when asked if there's a chance the tumor might reappear, Elizabeth promptly replied, "I'll slap the hell out of it if it does!"

The press had a field day covering Elizabeth's latest dance with doom and the tabloids had her hovering near death on many occasions. When she finally emerged from her recuperation to attend a dollhouse exhibit, the public was once

Elizabeth summed up her take on all her health crises and dangerous battles with addiction when she gleefully told Johnny Carson on her sixtieth birthday, "it's kind of astonishing that I made it!"

again stunned by her plucky luminescence. Her hair, which had been shaved for the operation, had grown back into a platinum crewcut, and Taylor decided to let nature take its course. The result was a chic, if slightly punk, new look. And most important of all, aside from an almost undetectable slower speech pattern (perhaps caused by the seizure medication), Taylor emerged physically unscathed.

Still, reports of her frailty are constantly written up in the press. In an interview with Barbara Walters, Elizabeth leapt out of her chair and did a quick little walk and shimmy to prove that she is far from an invalid. But she admitted to Walters that she had been laid up for more than a year after several falls and many broken bones, the most serious being a fractured back. Lying in bed, she became so depressed that she preferred to stay in her bedroom and never leave the house. It was a visit from her friend actor Rod Steiger, who had fought depression himself, that motivated her to get out of the doldrums and once again become enthused about life. She further claimed that all she wanted out of life was to keep feeling healthy and strong so she can travel wherever she is needed to support the AIDS cause.

As for acting, Elizabeth has stated that no one has been offering her parts because they're scared to insure her, and she maintains that being told she is no longer employable makes her even more eager to act. She is still receiving kudos from the film industry, though. Soon after her sixty-sixth birthday, the Screen Actors Guild honored her as the thirty-fourth recipient of their prestigious Life Achievement Award for her career accomplishments and humanitarian contributions as spokesperson and fund-raiser for AIDS awareness and research. She received a similar award in 1993 from the American Film Institute, and in 2000, she was presented with a British Film Institute fellowship, the equivalent of a lifetime achievement award. The country of her birth honored Taylor again in 2000 by granting her the highest compliment possible: Queen Elizabeth II made Taylor a Dame Commander of the Order of the British Empire in honor of her services to acting and charity. Describing the award as "the peak honor of my life," Dame Elizabeth, as she is now titled, fondly recalled Richard Burton, who had been awarded the OBE (Order of the British Empire) years earlier. "I miss him so much. I wish he was here," she confessed. Because of her two hip-replacement surgeries, she had to be supported by two of her sons as she came down the steps of Buckingham Palace. Dame Elizabeth was clearly proud and excited by the event, saying, "I can't believe it! Me! Getting a dameship!"

In 1998 her ex-husband Larry Fortensky, who had problems with the law after their divorce, fell down a flight of stairs in his home outside Los Angeles

OPPOSITE *Elizabeth clutches yet another Lifetime Achievement Award, this one from the British Academy Film Awards. Since England quarantines animals coming into the country, Elizabeth rarely visits her birthplace because her favorite traveling companion is her dog.*

In the mid-1990s, the commemorative awards began to rain down upon Elizabeth. She often claimed to agree with the critics in their assessment that she was not a very serious actress, but after viewing a video montage of her career, Taylor modestly asked, "I wasn't all that bad, was I?"

and was hospitalized in critical condition. His stumble was rumored to be the result of alcohol consumption. Although Fortensky had fought Elizabeth over their divorce settlement and demanded more money, she was genuinely concerned for his health and spoke to him on the phone while he was in the hospital after a tracheotomy and with a feeding tube in his stomach. After eight years of sharing her life with him, Elizabeth said, she could not just shut off her affection like a faucet—regardless of their differences. Then another emotional blow struck. Her life-long friend Roddy McDowall died of cancer. She was able to be with him during his final hours, which were no doubt extremely difficult for her. Indeed, when news of his death first broke, Elizabeth told reporters she could only express her deep shock.

While good friends such as Rod Steiger and singer-songwriter Carole Bayer-Sager are a great comfort to Taylor, she takes immense pride in her role not only as matriarch of the AIDS community, but of her own family, which

As a Hollywood veteran for over a half a century, Elizabeth has inevitably lost a lot of friends. When Roddy McDowall died in 1998, Elizabeth was devastated. He was not only her oldest friend, but a stalwart supporter who could always make her laugh at herself.

When asked what her tombstone should read, Elizabeth answered simply, "Here lies Elizabeth.... She Lived." Skimming over her long career and dramatic life experiences, Elizabeth's summation is an understatement.

includes nine grandchildren. It's a credit to Taylor as a mother that although her children were raised in a very unconventional atmosphere, they are all stable, independent individuals who do not seem to share their mother's extravagant tastes. Michael Wilding, Jr., lives near Taylor with his wife, Brooke, the daughter of actor Jack Palance. Christopher lives in Taos, New Mexico, near Elizabeth's brother, Howard. Although Christopher's ex-wife, Aileen, has been fighting full-blown AIDS since 1993, neither he nor their two sons have tested positive for the disease. Liza Todd lives in upstate New York with her artist husband and for many years has enjoyed success as a sculptor, specializing in horses. Maria Burton Carson is a married homemaker living in Manhattan, who in tribute to her doting, adoptive mother named her own daughter Elizabeth.

As Elizabeth ages, the inevitable reports about her health problems seem to escalate, but each time she has a setback the public and press alike are amazed at the vitality and strength she exudes at public engagements. It seems as if her many brushes with death over the years have only increased her appetite for life. Indeed, Elizabeth's perfume mantra, "I have a passion for life," is a fitting motto for her entire existence. Her dramatic personal life, which to her dismay has often overpowered her acting achievements, is being led on her own terms. A pampered star all her life, Elizabeth is no doubt headstrong but the more one learns about her, the more one comes to realize that she is essentially a deeply caring, frank human being. Underneath all the glitz, Elizabeth truly relishes life. Perhaps losing Mike Todd in her mid-twenties reinforced her sense of life's fragility. That tragic experience certainly added immense depth to her acting. But it may simply be that Elizabeth is a born fighter. Richard Burton often marveled at the paradox of her exterior vulnerability and interior steeliness. In an interview following her brain surgery, Elizabeth summed up her awe-inspiring fortitude with trademark candor: "I don't think I want to live to be ninety-nine, but I think sometimes I am indestructible."

CONCLUSION

"I'm not like anyone. . . . I'm me!"
—Taylor as Gloria Wandrous in
Butterfield 8 (1960)

There will never be another Elizabeth Taylor. She is one of the last of the true screen legends—a direct link to over a half century of American movie history. And yet she is so much more, most notably a humanitarian who has tirelessly raised millions of dollars for AIDS research and other charities. She is also a very savvy businesswoman, devoted mother, proud grandmother, great-grandmother, and loyal friend. To her millions of fans and even her detractors, Taylor is a woman of operatic dimensions, who has always managed, sometimes against catastrophic obstacles, to embrace life with admirable gusto and humor. She has truly earned her status as one of the twentieth century's most fascinating women.

opposite *Elizabeth Taylor, circa 1950.*

A Body of Work

FILMOGRAPHY

There's One Born Every Minute (1942) as Gloria Twine

Lassie Come Home (1943) as Priscilla

Jane Eyre (1944) as Helen Burns (uncredited)

The White Cliffs of Dover (1944) as young Betsy (uncredited)

National Velvet (1944) as Velvet Brown

Courage of Lassie (1946) as Kathie Merrick (also known as *Blue Sierra*)

Life with Father (1947) as Mary Skinner

Cynthia (1947) as Cynthia Bishop (also known as *Cynthia: The Rich, Full Life* and *The Rich Full Life*)

A Date with Judy (1948) as Carol Pringle

Julia Misbehaves (1948) as Susan Packett

Conspirator (1949) as Melinda Greyton

Little Women (1949) as Amy March

The Big Hangover (1950) as Mary Belney

Father of the Bride (1950) as Kay Banks

Quo Vadis? (1951) in a cameo role (uncredited)

Father's Little Dividend (1951) as Kay Banks Dunstan

A Place in the Sun (1951) as Angela Vickers

Callaway Went Thataway (1951) in a cameo role (also known as *The Star Said No*)

Ivanhoe (1952) as Rebecca

Love Is Better Than Ever (1952) as Anastasia Macaboy (also known as *The Light Fantastic*)

The Girl Who Had Everything (1953) as Jean Latimer

The Last Time I Saw Paris (1954) as Helen Ellswirth

Beau Brummell (1954) as Lady Patricia Belham

Rhapsody (1954) as Louise Durant

Elephant Walk (1954) as Ruth Wiley

Giant (1956) as Leslie Lynnton Benedict

Raintree County (1957) as Susanna Drake

Cat on a Hot Tin Roof (1958) as Maggie "The Cat" Pollitt

Suddenly, Last Summer (1959) as Catherine Holly

Butterfield 8 (1960) as Gloria Wandrous

Scent of Mystery (1960) as Sally Kennedy (uncredited cameo) (Also known as *Holiday in Spain*)

Cleopatra (1963) as Cleopatra

The V.I.P.s (1963) as Frances Andros (also known as *International Hotel*)

The Big Sur (1965) as herself (uncredited)

The Sandpiper (1965) as Laura Reynolds

Who's Afraid of Virginia Woolf? (1966) as Martha

Doctor Faustus (1967) as Helen of Troy

The Comedians (1967) as Martha Pineda

The Taming of the Shrew (1967) as Katharina (also known as *La Bisbetica domata*)

Reflections in a Golden Eye (1967) as Leonora Penderton

Secret Ceremony (1968) as Leonora

Boom! (1968) as Flora "Sissy" Goforth

The Only Game in Town (1970) as Fran Walker

Hammersmith Is Out (1972) as Jimmie Jean Jackson

X, Y, and Zee (1972) as Zee Blakeley (also known as *Zee and Co.*)

Under Milk Wood (1973) as Rosie Probert

Ash Wednesday (1973) as Barbara Sawyer

Night Watch (1973) as Ellen Wheeler

That's Entertainment! (1974) one of eleven narrators

The Driver's Seat (1973) as Lise (also known as *Identikit* and *Psychotic*)

The Blue Bird (1976) multiple roles as Queen of Light, Mother, Witch, and Maternal Love (also known as *Sinyaya ptitsa*)

A Little Night Music (1978) as Desiree Armfeldt

Winter Kills (1979) as Lola (uncredited)

The Mirror Crack'd (1980) as Marina Rudd

The Flintstones (1994) as Pearl Slaghoople

STAGE

Lillian Hellman's *The Little Foxes*, as Regina Giddens (USA and
    England, 1981)
Noël Coward's *Private Lives*, as Amanda Prynn (USA, 1983)

TELEVISION MOVIES

Divorce His/Divorce Hers (1973) as Jane Reynolds
Victory at Entebbe (1976) as Edra Vilnofsky
Between Friends (1983) as Deborah Shapiro (also known as
    Nobody Makes Me Cry)
Malice in Wonderland (1985) Louella O. Parsons (also known as
    The Rumor Mill)
North and South (1985) as Madam Conti
There Must Be a Pony (1986) as Marguerite Sydney
Poker Alice (1987) as Alice Moffit
Sweet Bird of Youth (1989) as Alexandra Del Lago

OTHER TELEVISION APPEARANCES

Elizabeth Taylor in London (1963)
The Lucy Show (1970)
All My Children (1970)
Return Engagement (1978)
Repeat Performance (1978)
General Hospital (1981)
Genocide (1981)
Montgomery Clift (1983)
A Concert for Life: A Tribute to Freddie Mercury (1992)
The Simpsons (1992, 1993)
Happy Birthday Elizabeth: A Celebration of Life (1997)

*A 1954 photo reflects an image of two
Elizabeths. Years later, when an
admirer gushed that there was "only
one Elizabeth Taylor," Elizabeth
quickly exclaimed, "Thank God for that!"*

INDEX

PHOTO CREDITS

Every effort has been made to ascertain and correctly credit the copyright holders and/or owners for all images appearing in this book. The publisher will correct mistaken credits and include any omitted credits in all future editions.